AF599063

MURDER & MAYHEM IN GALLATIN COUNTY, MONTANA

MURDER & MAYHEM IN GALLATIN COUNTY, MONTANA

KELLY SUZANNE HARTMAN
with contributions by the Gallatin Historical Society
and Gallatin History Museum

Published by The History Press
Charleston, SC
www.historypress.com

Copyright © 2021 by Kelly Suzanne Hartman
All rights reserved

First published 2021

Manufactured in the United States

ISBN 9781467149143

Library of Congress Control Number: 2021943435

Notice: The information in this book is true and complete to the best of our knowledge. It is offered without guarantee on the part of the author or The History Press. The author and The History Press disclaim all liability in connection with the use of this book.

All rights reserved. No part of this book may be reproduced or transmitted in any form whatsoever without prior written permission from the publisher except in the case of brief quotations embodied in critical articles and reviews.

The truth, however ugly in itself, is always curious and beautiful to seekers after it.
—*Agatha Christie,* The Murder of Roger Ackroyd

Thus ends the story…and its tragedy. Each man had his friends, each has his defenders. Possibly one may have been too jealous, too revengeful; possibly the other was too hasty…whether friend or foe the verdict of all is recorded in one brief sentence, "It's too bad."
—Anaconda Standard, *September 16, 1900*

CONTENTS

INTRODUCTION

Murder & Mayhem in Gallatin County, Montana is a book I never thought I would be writing; as many would attest, I am a complete baby when it comes to anything remotely gruesome. Yet here I am, with a book filled with crimes from axe murders to old-west shootouts. My interest in these topics began when I started working as the first curator at the Gallatin History Museum, which still houses a built-in gallows. To reconcile walking under it daily, I learned the story behind the only man executed there and wrote *Murder Along the Yellowstone Trail: The Execution of Seth Danner*. I learned, through my research, that the climax of a story, the murder itself, is not really the climax at all. Because human nature is drawn to the continuing drama, the victim is often lost after the initial reporting of a murder. All the attention drifts to the one to be punished, the plight of the accused. The victim often turns nameless, awash in the details of the murder. If one thinks about the plot construction of an Agatha Chirstie murder mystery, the murder occurs in the first third of a book; the rest of the novel is trying to understand motive, means and punishment.

I have written the stories in this book as though they were happening right now. I want to pull my readers along on a journey as the story is uncovered, much like readers of local papers at the time would have discovered the details of a crime or how detectives and authorities would uncover the mystery. In this formatting, one can see the misconceptions, mistakes and wrong turns made during an investigation. Sometimes the crimes are cut-and-dry; sometimes they are so convoluted one feels like they are in a room of mirrors trying to find the right path forward. This, I believe, is what makes murder mysteries so interesting. It is human nature to try to understand, to feel the fog lift and to see the puzzle pieces fall into place. Perhaps that is why the unsolved are so fascinating: the pieces are still out there to be gathered and put together.

The execution of Seth Danner is laid out in brief in this book; with only three legal executions in the county, I couldn't leave him out. I think the most interesting part of having come from his story to this book is how the fate of the convicted differs so widely. Seth had little chance of escaping the crime he was accused of, one I believe he may have paid for unjustly, but one should observe closely how rarely others share his end. Realizing this led me to question, over and over again, Why was his crime considered more serious? Why was he not given the benefit of any doubt? I put his story last so that if you read this book front to back, you can truly see the potential inequality with which his case was handled.

I composed the book from a long list of murders that have occurred in the Gallatin Valley. As such, there are many that were left out. I looked for stories that had gray areas, stories that lead one to question if they caught the right person for the crime. Trying to find humor in murder is difficult, but surprisingly, it is there, particularly in the ridiculous stories people make up to avoid punishment or to put the blame on others, farces that are often seen straight through as fiction. There is also great sadness, including for the perpetrators of the crime, who often feel remorse over their actions, which can never be undone once they have been committed. Some of them lose their lives literally on the gallows or figuratively by life imprisonment due to the life they have taken, and some suffer the consequences for a crime they may never have committed. Again, the drama is in the aftermath, what comes next once murder is discovered.

The murders in this book occurred primarily between the 1880s and the early 1940s. The jail records and murder files at the Gallatin Historical Society were my starting points for research. I then used a variety of resources, including the wonderful collection of newspapers at the historical society, digitized papers on Chronicling America and Newspapers.com, the society's family research files, Ancestry.com, the Montana Memory Project's prison records from the Montana Historical Society and other various jail records at the Gallatin History Museum, to tell the full stories.

I would like to thank the Gallatin Historical Society and Museum for letting me use their vast amount of historic resources on this project and my curatorial assistant, Victoria Richard, whose help researching and scouring newspapers was invaluable.

Now enter the world of confusion and clarity, lies and unknown truths, murder and mayhem in Gallatin County.

Chapter 1

DISAGREEABLE PARTIES

MURDER IN SELF-DEFENSE

I am glad now that they have got me, so that I will get it off my mind.
—Joe Reiser, second-degree murder, 1915

The setup: two parties involved in a lively discussion—maybe too lively. A threat is heard, sometimes more than once. One of the parties is found dead; witnesses take the stand saying the threats were substantiated. The accused has only one thing in his favor: the deceased attacked him first, so he had to react. It was self-defense. The witnesses to the crime are confused, or there are none at all; no one can say who threw the first punch. What does one believe?

On Saturday August 16, 1913, Jess C. Crago, an engineer at the Three Forks Portland cement works, was shot dead in the town of Trident. His killer was Domenico Romeo, who had been working under Crago at the cement works. The two men had a rocky working relationship. It seems Crago had chided Romeo several times about the "careless manner in which he did his work," to which Romeo had replied with obstinance. Prior to going to work that day, Romeo had been drinking heavily and stated to others that he was either going to quit or "get" Crago. When the engineer Crago mentioned something about his work to Romeo during his shift, the latter asked for a fight. Crago stated he didn't want to fight but did want Romeo to do his work. This enraged Romeo, who quickly pulled a revolver from his pocket and fired. The bullet hit Crago in his stomach, coming out his neck (for the bullet to have taken such a trajectory, the logistics of which were never fully disclosed, Romeo must have been either on the ground or downhill from Crago). The man was rushed to Helena for an operation but died hours later, having made an antemortem statement. Romeo fled into the hills, where he was soon discovered and taken to Three Forks. Deputy Sheriff Copenhaver brought the man to the Gallatin County jail in Bozeman over the Gallatin Valley railroad. The following two days were spent gathering evidence in both Trident and Helena to build a case against Romeo while Crago's body was sent to Missoula, where his family resided. He left a wife and four small children as well as a homestead in Trident.[1]

An interesting aspect to the case was the time period. The recently passed Alien Gun Law prevented noncitizens from having a firearm in their possession. The arrest and charge of Romeo of first-degree murder prompted the deputy game warden of Townsend to make a thorough search of the Italian quarter of Trident, known derogatorily as Dagotown. Two revolvers and one stiletto had been found, and the violators had been prosecuted.[2]

While the charge against Romeo had been publicized, his arraignment would be postponed until an Italian interpreter could be found. The trial would not be placed on the docket until November 10, 1913. Romeo would be defended by George D. Pease, with Attorney Justin M. Smith for the prosecution. Crago's widow would attend all the sessions with her three-year-old daughter.

The charge against Romeo was first-degree murder, and the defense was entering a plea of self-defense. A witness for the state and worker at the plant, Joseph Romeo (no relation to Domenico Romeo), testified through an interpreter what he saw the day of the murder. According to Joseph, he saw Crago grab a sledgehammer during the quarrel between the two men with the intent of striking Romeo with it when the latter fired his gun. According to the manager of the plant, who also testified, he had not heard before of any disagreement between the two men, who worked closely together, as Romeo had been employed to help Crago at the plant. Robert Seabald, who was the first on the scene, testified to finding Crago, who cried out to him, "Bob, I'm shot!" When Seabald went to the scene of the crime, he found Joseph Romeo, who told him, "Dey make shoot!" Another man testified to hearing the shot and then arriving to find Domenico Romeo with a smoking gun while Joseph Romeo was running away.[3]

While the trial continued, a legal question was raised. One morning one of the jurors had not arrived at court. A bailiff had been sent to retrieve him and found him dead in his bed. It was rumored that the man suffered

Cement plant at Trident, 1915. *Gallatin Historical Society/Gallatin History Museum.*

from epileptic fits, which may have been the cause of death. No foul play was suspected, but it did raise a question: Could the trial continue, or would a new jury need to be chosen? In the end it was decided the jury had to be dismissed and a new one called up.[4]

The new session would begin in early December with an entirely new jury. The testimony would be a duplication of that which had been laid out in November, giving little for the *Weekly Courier* to discuss this time. On December 16, 1913, it was announced that Romeo had been found guilty of second-degree murder and that it would be a few days before he would "learn how long he must live in Deer Lodge." The prosecution relied on the three statements made by Crago prior to his death that all stated that Romeo had shot him. This was set against the word of Romeo, who had stated to many people that Crago had struck at him first, so he had fired. On the stand, Domenico Romeo testified to having no problems with Crago until August 3, when Crago's brother had arrived. Crago wanted his brother to have Romeo's job, according to Romeo. From then on, things had been tense between the two men, culminating in threats that Crago would kill Romeo if Romeo did not leave his job for Crago's brother. On the day of the incident, Romeo had been an hour late to work, telling a coworker, Gianni, that he

Domenico Romeo, second-degree murder, 1913, prison, Deer Lodge, Montana. *Montana Historical Society*.

would not go to work that day, as Crago wanted him gone. Gianni convinced Romeo to go on his shift and ask the foreman if he could be transferred when he planned to leave that fall, per Crago's request. The latter was not happy to see Romeo arriving late and chastised him for it, physically shoving Romeo. The quarrel ensued with Joseph Romeo watching. According to the *Weekly Courier*, "Attorney Pease upon the testimony of the three Italians, Domenico Romeo, Joseph Romeo, and Gianni, built up a defense which he placed before the jury in logical and masterly style in his final argument of two hours." It seemed to the defense that had Romeo been planning to kill Crago, he would have had plenty of opportunity either on shift with the man or to search him out at his homestead, where no one would be around. Furthermore, if Romeo had truly planned murder that day, he would have fled directly into the hills to avoid being seen near Crago with the gun. But he did not seek Crago out in a secluded place, nor did he flee directly after the event; instead, he had changed his clothes for work, had the argument, and shot Crago. Because he had been seen, he left to change clothes in the commotion and then, deciding the seemingly best course to take in this instance, fled the scene into the surrounding hills. In the end, the jury was out for six hours before returning their verdict of murder in the second, clearly believing much of Romeo's story.[5]

The penalty, while not death, was fairly steep at life imprisonment. Domenico Romeo was given a forty-year sentence of hard labor at Deer Lodge State Prison. At the time of his sentencing, Romeo was twenty-eight years old. The judge stated, "Personally I do not believe that Crago held the sledge in his hand at the time. I believe that sledge was an afterthought," making it clear he did not believe the murder had been justified. As the penalty had been left to the judge by the jury, the stiff sentence was all his decision. According to intake records at Deer Lodge, Domenico Romeo was married, with his wife, Maria Romeo, still living in Italy. It is unknown if he spent his whole sentence at Deer Lodge or what became of him after prison.[6]

An interesting case involved two Hungarian friends whose relationship turned sinister on Christmas Eve 1915. Joe Fink and Joe Reiser had come to America about 1900, continuing their already established friendship. They had worked as farmhands in Minnesota and were looking for employment in the Bozeman area. It seems they had taken turns paying the bills, depending on who could find employment. All testimony showed that the two men were the best of friends. Together they had rented a cabin from William Wademan, which is where, on Christmas Eve, one nude body was found terribly mutilated in the cellar. The hunt for the murderer started off poorly. For roughly a week, authorities were on the lookout for the wrong man. A boardinghouse in Butte messed up the names of the two men, leading to a search for the victim, Joe Fink, instead of the supposed murderer.[7]

For days, the only tip in the search for the missing man was that a person of his description had boarded the train from Salesville to Bozeman and that upon his arrival, he had asked where the Northern Pacific depot was located. Finally on December 31, Joe Reiser, as he was now discovered to be, was captured at Dickinson, North Dakota. He was discovered while attempting to withdraw funds deposited by Joe Fink at the First National Bank in Cando. Interestingly, Joe Fink's body was being sent that same day to roughly the same area, St. Paul, at the request of the Austro-Hungarian consulate because a relative of his had been found in that city and requested the body for burial.[8]

The murder would be labeled by the *Bozeman Weekly Courier* as "brutal beyond belief." It would come out that Joe Fink had been murdered with an axe, apparently hacked and beaten to death. The motive remained mysterious throughout the inquest, and it was not until Reiser was caught that a greater understanding of what occurred came out. When apprehended, Reiser had seemed relieved and had gone straight to bed when he arrived in Bozeman, completely worn out. One should note that Sheriff Del Gray found the man in fine physical condition, with no signs of any fight on his person. From what Reiser told of his story, signs should still have shown ten days after Christmas Eve. According to Reiser, following words the night before, at three o'clock that morning, Fink had suddenly pulled the blankets from Reiser and struck him. When Reiser struck back, Fink had grabbed a shotgun and fired, missing the former due to Reiser's quick movement. Here Reiser said he was able to throw Fink to the floor but that the shotgun had come down hard on his arm, almost paralyzing it. When he asked Fink to stop, he stated Fink said, "Joe, you got to die." As the struggle continued, Fink picked up an axe, more fists were thrown and eventually Fink had Reiser about the neck and was choking him. It was then that Reiser had gotten hold of the axe and hit Fink again and again; for, he stated, the man had continued to rise multiple times during the attack, so he had to keep swinging.[9]

Sheriff Del E. Gray, 1915–19. *Gallatin Historical Society/ Gallatin History Museum.*

While confessing, Reiser seemed completely remorseful for the deed. He had been scared at first, gathering all he could to leave town right away. While in Dickinson, he had wanted to go to a doctor for his arm but had been dissuaded by the high cost of a prescription. Reiser stated that he had "not slept any since that awful night, and Joe's face is before me all the time....I am glad now that they have got me, so that I will get it off my mind." It seems he had wanted to give himself up multiple times, but something had kept pushing him to run. His first instinct to run had been prompted by his belief that a mob might hang him before he got a chance to explain what had happened.[10]

The trial took place in February 1916, and Reiser secured his own attorney for his defense and took the stand on his own behalf. In the courtroom, he was on the stand for three hours to tell his story while the bloodstained bed (it is unclear if the entire bed or just the sheets were present), shotgun and axe were all laid before him. Reiser even acted out some of the fighting that had occurred. While the motive may have been self-defense, it was never clear, at least by what the media covered, what the fighting had all been about.[11]

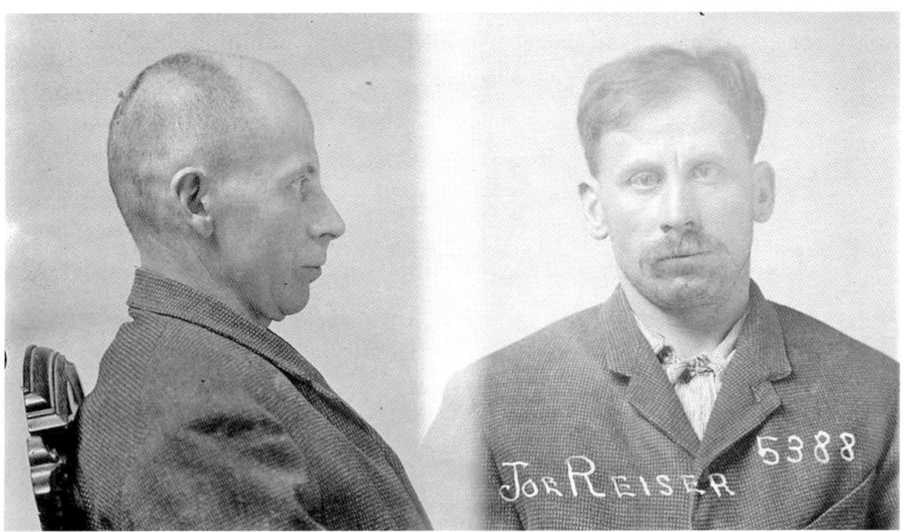

Joe Reiser, second-degree murder, 1916, prison, Deer Lodge, Montana. *Montana Historical Society*.

On February 28, Reiser was convicted of second-degree murder and sentenced to not less than forty nor more than fifty years in prison. The jury had wished clemency in the matter; however, Judge B.B. Law had not fully accepted Reiser's plea of self-defense, believing the motive to have been robbery. The judge noted that Reiser had not shown mercy to Fink, to which Reiser replied, "All I can say is that I had to fight for life." It is unknown what happened to Joe Reiser following his prison sentence, although the thirty-eight-year-old man would have been at least seventy-eight upon his release if he served the shortest time from his sentence.[12]

In February 1917, the bodies of George S. Miller and Gladstone Stevens were discovered frozen in Gallatin Canyon. Both had been shot. Andrew Levinski was sought for the murders by Sheriff Del Gray. The trouble had begun over ownership of mining claims. It seems Levinski had threatened Thomas Michener, whose claims Miller and Stevens were associated with, on multiple occasions over twenty-five years, but Michener had never taken these threats seriously.[13]

Levinski surrendered himself at Karst's Camp, the search for him having been a futile one. It had been his intention to give himself up since the shootings had occurred. It seems he had almost immediately gotten to a phone to contact his attorney about what had happened, stating that he intended to come quietly. This was twenty hours prior to the discovery of the murders and the news reaching town. When Levinski's attorney read about the murders and the search for the killer in the papers, he telephoned the sheriff to let him know Levinski was waiting at Karst Camp to be picked up. According to the attorney, after he had received the call from Levinski, he had felt it too late to call the sheriff so had thought it better to wait till morning; however, the matter "completely slipped his mind," and he forgot about it until he saw the newspaper article.[14]

Levinski's bail, fixed at $35,000, was furnished, allowing the man to be at liberty pending trial. The bodies of Miller and Stevens were hard to get to; as the roads were impassable by automobile, sleds had to be used. The recovery party was only able to make two miles per hour through snow four to ten feet deep over the ten miles to the Levinski cabin, where the bodies still lay. The men's horses still stood tied up to trees where they had been three days in four feet of snow. Thus, the inquest and coroner's verdict would take extra time to pass. Levinski had admitted right away to the murders, pleading self-defense, but two counts of first-degree murder were filed by courty attorney C.E. Carlson.[15]

The Levinski trial began on June 12, 1917. The principal witnesses for the prosecution testified on the confession from Levinski himself, those who had been at the scene of the crime afterward and those who had heard Levinski use threatening language. The prosecution started its story on December 31, when Miller, Stevens and a man named Sam Kratteer visited Levinski to close a deal on copper mines that Levinski owned. During a long conversation in which no terms could be agreed on, Miller and Stevens had excused themselves from the cabin for a spell. Upon their return, Levinski had questioned their doings, but they claimed to have done nothing while away. The next morning Levinski found they had posted location notices at the mine. He had become enraged and had started for Bozeman to talk to a lawyer. It was testified that following that altercation, Levinski had told the lawyer that he would have killed the lot had they not had the drop on him, and he was glad he did not because Kratteer, whom Levinski thought was innocent, was among them.[16]

The prosecution attempted to discredit Levinski's account of the day of the murders. In Levinski's statement, he had said he knew the men were Michener's lot due to his dog being with them; however, the prosecution went on to state that Michener had his dogs with him that day. The prosecution also tried to discredit his assertion of how many times he had shot each man and how the gun duel had gone down. According to Levinski, he had arrived home from cutting wood on January 29 to find men and a dog near his cabin. As he had entered his cabin, one had taken a shot at him. From the cabin, he had shot one man and then had broken a window and shot through there back and forth at the second man who had taken cover. Evidence of these bullets had been difficult to find in the snow at the time, and the prosecution used this to discredit Levinski's story. It was then related how Levinski had admitted his guilt right away to Sheriff Gray upon meeting him at Karst, stating, "I am sorry to cause you all this trouble, but I had to do it." Levinski himself had told how the second man had started getting up after being hit the first time and how he had shot him a second time. He felt remorse at this, saying, "I am sorry I shot that last time. It wasn't necessary, but then I thought he was going to shoot at me." According to a witness for the prosecution, a gun had not been found where the second man lay although shells were. Mrs. Karst stated that Levinski said, "I have come to give myself up. I've left meat in the hills."[17] The prosecution would also attempt to discredit Levinski's story by claiming Nelson Story Jr. "bought evidence" to secure Levinki's acquittal.

The case was given to the jury for consideration on June 17 after nearly a week of trial. The jury was only out three hours before bringing back a verdict of not guilty. Levinski was set free without even a charge of manslaughter. It seems his story, which never wavered, and his testimony on the stand, which

Levinski Cabin. *Gallatin Historical Society/Gallatin History Museum.*

had been unshakable, had stood true for the jury. Since the call was for first-degree murder only, Levinski could not be held on any other charge.[18]

On January 21, 1920, it was reported that Francis Huffine lay in critical condition in the Bozeman Deaconess Hospital while Elmer Nunnelly awaited the outcome. Nunnelly would be charged with assault if Huffine lived and first-degree murder if he did not. This dire situation had begun as a quarrel over a sleigh that had been lent between two brothers. It seems Francis Huffine had lent his brother Fielder Huffine a sleigh some time in the past. On the day of the shooting, Francis had gone to his brother's ranch to retrieve either the sleigh or money for it but met with Nunnelly, as Fielder was out of town. Nunnelly had consulted Fielder's wife on the matter, and it had been decided that it should rest until Fielder returned. Francis was asked to leave, and a fight ensued. The women on the ranch, including Fielder's wife, watched the fight for quite some time, even removing a knife from Francis's hand before he could use it on Nunnelly. Both men were battered and bruised when a shot was fired. Neither of the women saw the shooting.[19]

Huffine, who believed himself to be dying, detailed the affray to Attorney Farris at the hospital. According to Francis, the fighting had started almost immediately when Nunnelly had cursed him and knocked him down. A piece of plank wielded by Nunnelly was fought over, but eventually both parties had agreed to stop. The *Bozeman Courier* would report that as they got up Nunnelly told Francis, "I just guess I'll kill you, you ——." Nunnelly had then reached for a gun in the sleigh, and Francis had walked toward him, finding it useless to try to run. Nunnelly had then shot him point-blank across his stomach. Another fight had begun over the gun, but weakened by the wound, Francis soon acquiesced. Nunnelly had pointed the gun at Francis, but Fielder's wife prevented it. Francis had been taken to his own home but was quickly transferred to Bozeman due to the severity of his wound. Sheriff Charles Esgar retrieved Nunnelly with no trouble at Fielder Huffine's ranch.[20]

Three days following the shooting, Francis Huffine died. Nunnelly had been kept in the jail awaiting this news and his fate. Francis's dying statements, that Nunnelly had been the aggressor, seemed damning. Nunnelly entered a plea of not guilty and was released on a $15,000 bail to await trial in March.[21]

The first day of the trial, which began on March 1, was taken with the selection of the jury. Interestingly, this was the third murder trial involving a shotgun to be held in two months at Gallatin County. The trials of Richard

Huffine Ranch on Springhill, 1953. *Gallatin Historical Society/Gallatin History Museum.*

Ward and Fred Dambres (see chapter 5) preceded the trial of Nunnelly. This latest case was wrapped up on March 6, and Nunnelly walked away a free man. Nunnelly's story at the trial was more detailed than the previous accounts published in the papers. According to Nunnelly, Huffine had been coming at him around the sleigh with a knife when he, Nunnelly, fired at him. He stated that although he had at first pointed the gun at Huffine's head, he had lowered it because he just wanted to stop the man from attacking him, not kill him.[22]

Arch Martin, who had taken Francis home after the shooting, was questioned about the character of the man. According to Martin, Francis was violent and quarrelsome with a "reputation for using a knife." It seems the man had had disputes with much of the neighborhood. Another witness would testify that Francis's reputation for truth was bad. Those who saw Nunnelly after the fight testified to his bloodied head. According to the defense, Nunnelly had not been angry when he had returned from consulting Mrs. Fielder Huffine, and if Francis's dying testimony was to be believed, then many of these witnesses had lied on the stand. The defense even used Nunnelly's background as a soldier as evidence for his defense, stating that "any man who had been a soldier...would naturally try to uphold the laws of the country for which he had fought." Apparently, the defense put up a winning fight since Nunnelly was acquitted of the charge. Elmer Nunnelly passed away at age sixty-two in 1948, and his grave in Mountain View Cemetery in Livingston, Montana, is marked with a military headstone.[23]

Perhaps one of the oddest murder weapons in the history of Gallatin County, and maybe even in the history of murders in general, was that of the potato masher used to kill Andrew Clostad in 1931. The man was found unconscious from a severe beating, dying the same evening of his attack at a hospital in Bozeman. Two men—J.F. Shipman, aged sixty-six, and William (Shorty) Slining, aged forty-eight—were arrested for the crime. Both would plead self-defense, stating that Clostad had called Slining to his house, which the former rented from the latter. It seems Slining had been having difficulty getting his due rent from Clostad and had just days before talked to Sheriff O.L. DeVore, asking him to remove Clostad from the house. DeVore had told him the procedure necessary for removal, which Slining found too expensive. Many in the town had heard and would testify to Slining's threats to kill Clostad. Many would also testify that Clostad claimed he held a note that Slining owed him money. That evening, Slining had arrived with a wooden potato masher in hand and with Shipman in tow.[24]

At 1:30 a.m., Slining arrived at the police station, informing officers that he had just seen Clostad lying in his house, apparently injured. Officers called Deputy Sheriff Walton, and together they arrived at the house. The door was locked, but Slining, since he owned the place, opened the door with his key. There they found Clostad lying behind a stove in a pool of blood as well as blood smeared on the walls. An attempt to wake the man proved unproductive, and he was quickly rushed to the hospital in a dire state.

Potato masher used to kill Andrew Clostad, 1931. *Gallatin Historical Society/Gallatin History Museum.*

Portrait of the Huffine family, circa 1905. *Gallatin Historical Society/Gallatin History Museum.*

During this chaos, Shipman entered the room proclaiming that he had beat Clostad with a potato masher, which he then displayed for the officers. Both Slining and Shipman were taken into custody immediately.[25]

Clostad would die of his wounds soon after arriving at the hospital, leaving doctors to examine the death blows. According to one physician, there had been ten to twelve blows, most of which on their own would have been sufficient to cause death. The two men would be charged with first-degree murder and would be held in the county jail pending trial. The trial itself would be interesting, as the men would be tried together, not in separate cases. The attorney for the defense, Seth Bohart, would tell the jury that Slining was an "uneducated person, whose ordinary sense" had prevented him from paying the note he owned to Clostad, while Shipman was a "man of high moral character" who had willing given himself up, ready to face the consequences. Throughout the trial, both defendants would swear that Slining never struck Clostad. Evidence showed, however, that the blows on Clostad's head were of two varieties, one star shaped and one incised, indicating two different tools had been used in the beating.[26]

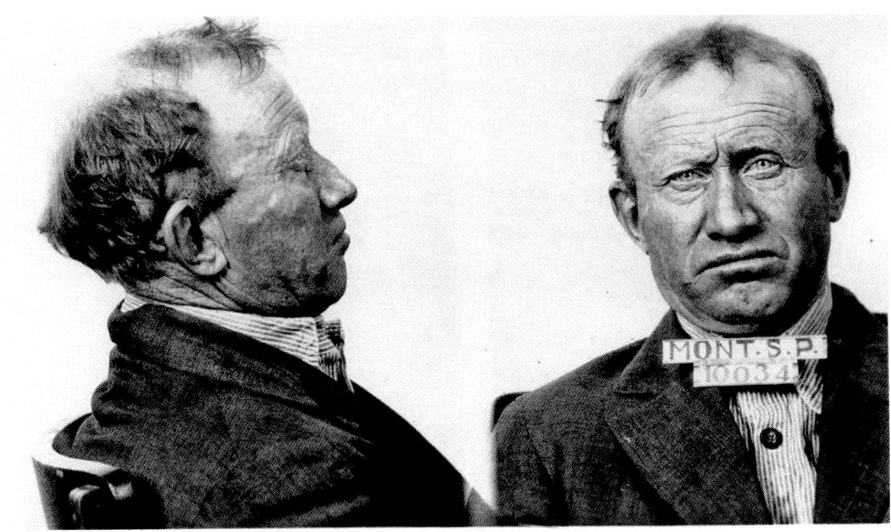

William (Shorty) Slining, manslaughter, 1931, prison, Deer Lodge, Montana. *Montana Historical Society.*

In any event, neither man would be found guilty of first-degree murder. Both were charged with manslaughter, as their testimony of self-defense seems to have been persuasive. Shipman received a sentence of ten years and Slining eight years at the state prison. Judge B.B. Law, however, had not been as persuaded and gave Shipman the maximum of ten years and Slining eight, stating that the evidence had revealed the men had "not acted solely in self-defense."[27]

Shipman returned to Bozeman upon his release, passing away at the age of ninety-one. It is unknown what happened to Slining, although in 1944 a William Slining did pass away at Deer Lodge, whether in the prison or on parole or neither is hard to say.

A few years later, on September 2, 1934, Dan Holland shot and killed Frank Sparlin with a shotgun blast to the face. The case was cut-and-dry despite Holland's attempts at pleading self-defense. According to the only witness, a Miss Emma Pritchard, Sparlin and she had arrived at the ranch, which she owned, to have a talk with Holland. Prichard had requested that her brother-in-law Sparlin help her with some legal matters, including some papers Holland wanted her to sign. When they arrived, Holland wanted to show Sparlin some recently threshed wheat. When they had returned from the barn to the car where Pritchard was waiting, she saw Holland had a shotgun at Sparlin's back; neither had had the gun when they had gone in, and she had not heard any loud disagreement or anything at all. She quickly removed herself from the car to stand aside, and when Sparlin went to get into the car seat and half turned his head, Holland had fired on him, killing him instantly. Following the murder, Holland had gone to Gallatin Gateway to telephone Undersheriff Isbell to come, not saying what had happened. When Isbell arrived, Holland was not back yet, but Pritchard laid out what had occurred. Isbell called for a coroner and someone to take Pritchard home and then waited for Holland, who soon arrived. Holland detailed what had happened, claiming the act was self-defense, although it was not clear why he had felt threatened. Before being taken to Bozeman, he asked to shave, and permission was granted.[28]

It seems Sparlin had been warned by E.F. Bunker, Miss Pritchard's attorney, about going to see Holland without an officer; he thought something serious might happen. It seems he had been right. The only witness called on at the inquest was Miss Pritchard, who told the exact same story she had to Undersheriff Isbell. The coroner's jury quickly brought back a verdict that Dan Holland had inflicted the wounds that had caused Sparlin's death. Holland would immediately be placed under custody pending his trial. It was believed that Attorney Fred Lay would ask for the death penalty in his prosecution of the case. Prior to the trial, Holland would receive new council when his attorney George Pease became severely ill and was unable to continue with the case.[29]

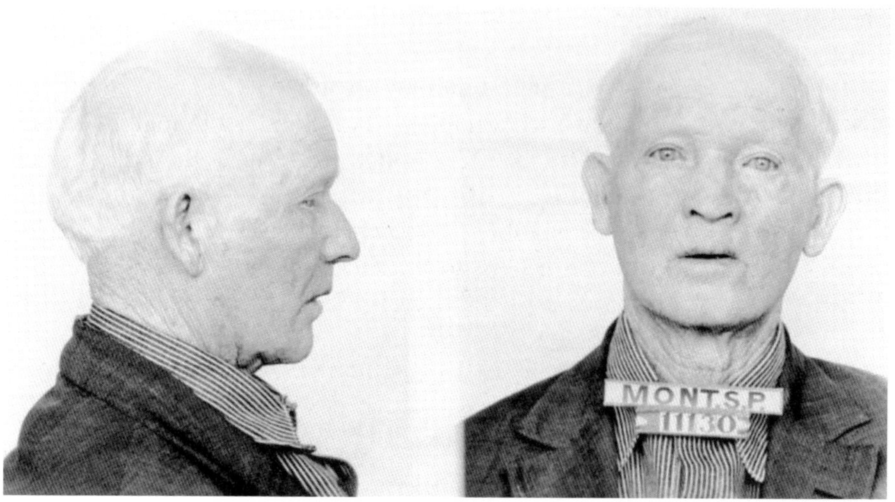

Dan Holland, first-degree murder, 1934, prison, Deer Lodge, Montana. *Montana Historical Society.*

The trial began in November, and according to Sheriff Lovitt Westlake, Holland had been unmoved since the murder had taken place. This was leading the defense, in lieu of any real motive for the killing, to discuss a plea of insanity in the case. This attempt did not hold, however, as both Dr. Seitz of Bozeman and Dr. Gladys Holmes of Warm Springs Asylum, experts brought in by the prosecution, believed Holland to be in full possession of his faculties at the time of the murder. It was also clear that Sparlin had been unarmed at the time, although Holland stated that he believed from the way Sparlin was getting into the car that he was going for a gun.[30]

The jury made quick work of the verdict, declaring Holland guilty of murder in the first degree in just an hour. It seems Holland was "badly shaken" at this pronouncement and had to be assisted out of the courtroom. Holland would be sentenced to life imprisonment at Deer Lodge. In passing the sentence, Jude Benjamin E. Berg stated: "Your days on this earth are numbered. Those days might well be spent by you in making peace with your Maker." At the time of the murder, Dan Holland was seventy years old. He would serve a shortened sentence of merely two months, for he would pass away in prison on January 29, 1935, just four days after his seventy-first birthday.[31]

Chapter 2

UNREQUITED LOVE

CRIMES OF PASSION

My God, Mary, were you hit?
—Walter Anderson, manslaughter, 1915

Crimes of passion are one of the most interesting types of murders. While the motive is clear, it is also so very unclear logically. The murder never really solves anything, and the reward, even if the killer gets away with it, is rarely a reward at all. Remorse almost inevitably follows. The murder of the loved one's lover is never going to gain the murderer the love he or she craves. It is a lose-lose scenario, which is why so often these crimes end as a murder-suicide.

On July 18, 1898, William Russell, his daughter and a man named John Russell arrived in town, registering at the Northern Pacific Hotel. R.T. Sloan, married to William Russell's daughter, also arrived with a friend, Earl Denny, and registered at the same hotel. The proprietor was somehow alerted to potential trouble, prompting him to talk with Russell about his concerns, to which Russell said there would not be an issue. The following morning Sloan and his friend Denny went to the Trivoli for a drink, followed soon by Russell. A quarrel between father and son-in-law immediately ensued and escalated quickly into a fight. Sloan pulled out a revolver, which he had purchased the previous evening, and shot his father-in-law through the stomach. Russell managed to run from the bar and into Rea & Co.'s store nearby before falling on the floor, announcing that he was shot and asking for someone to get a doctor and notify his daughter.[32]

Guy House Hotel, later the Northern Pacific Hotel. *Gallatin Historical Society/Gallatin History Museum.*

Russell was soon moved to a room in the Northern Pacific where a doctor tried everything he could to save the man to no avail. He passed away within four hours. Sloan did not wait around to be apprehended but also did not head for the hills immediately. It was said that following the shooting, he had stepped back up to the bar and finished his drink of whiskey before Denny and he left on horseback. Sheriff W.J. Fransham was quickly notified, and a posse was assembled to follow the men. At 10:00 a.m., Deputy Johnson found Sloan about three miles from Belgrade. Sloan was asked to surrender, which he promptly did; however, Denny was not captured, as the two had parted ways.[33]

No one really knew the motive for the shooting, but it was supposed that marital issues may have been the problem. It was rumored that Russell had brought his daughter to town for the purpose of filing divorce papers against Sloan. Those who knew Sloan found the incident surprising; it seems Sloan was never known to quarrel in the way he had with Russell. Russell was buried at the Bozeman Cemetery, and Sloan's trial was immediately set for the following week.[34]

On November 12, Sloan was found guilty of second-degree murder. During the trial, the courtroom had been packed, the case being "hotly contested" by many in the town. While Russell had been a well-known local rancher, Sloan was the adopted son of another well-known rancher, making the case of local concern. Sloan would be sentenced to fifteen years' imprisonment, although an appeal was immediately sent to the Supreme Court of Montana.[35]

A look at divorce papers signed in September 1898 shows that Carrie Sloan, formerly Carrie Russell, claimed Rolland Sloan had beaten her and spoke vile profanity toward her person. She claimed this had happened on numerous occasions although exact dates were unknown. It is also unknown whether this divorce was granted or if Sloan even went to Deer Lodge prison following the outcome of his appeal.

One of the most shocking types of murder is that of the murder-suicide, perhaps because there is little chance to process the damage. Unlike a typical murder where the perpetrator goes on trial, there is no one left to reconcile the loss. On January 16, 1900, in an article titled "Double Tragedy," it was reported that the sheriff in Bozeman had been alerted to two deaths that had occurred in Belgrade. With little more to go on, a team including a coroner set out on the westbound train. It soon came out that the two bodies were those of Mrs. Etta Davis, a boardinghouse keeper, and Frank Rogers, a merchant. Upon investigation by the Sheriff's Department, it was discovered that both had been killed with a Smith & Wesson .44-caliber revolver. It seems Rogers had been in dire financial straits due to a penchant for gambling, having recently lost his store to creditors. He was three months behind in his rent to Davis as well. When found, he had a bottle of unopened strychnine in his pocket, indicating he had planned either murder or suicide in the future. For whatever reason, he chose to use a gun instead. Rumors were that he had been drinking heavily for days and that his clerk had purchased a revolver for him only recently. It seems Rogers had been acquainted with the Davises from their hometown in North Carolina prior to coming west.[36]

Mrs. Davis had been shot in the back of the head by her ear, while Rogers had taken the gun to his own temple. A hired girl had been asleep in a chair in the sitting room but had not heard the shots, only the sound of something falling in the kitchen, which she hadn't investigated. She had been in the kitchen at about 10:00 p.m. when Rogers had walked in. When Mr. Davis, just back from Butte, discovered them, it was four o'clock in the morning. The *Avant Courier* was cryptic in stating that when he found them, Mr. Davis had not known they were dead. He had immediately taken their children, ages five and three, to the train station. The children would be placed with Mrs. Davis's sister-in-law, Mrs. Reverend Rickman of Bozeman. The act seemed to have no motive other than temporary insanity due to heavy drinking.[37]

However, the story would unfold differently in papers beyond Bozeman. On January 16, the *Anaconda Standard* printed a lengthy article on the matter titled "Rogers' Love Was Blind." According to this special

Downtown Belgrade, Montana, 1910. *Gallatin Historical Society/Gallatin History Museum.*

dispatch from Bozeman to the *Standard*, and not published in the local Bozeman paper, both Mr. Davis and Rogers had grown up with Etta and been suitors for her hand. Etta chose Davis; however, they had all remained cordial. The Davises had moved to Montana, and Mr. Davis had found employment with the *Bozeman Chronicle*. Rogers was persuaded to move west as well, and eventually, Mr. Davis and Rogers, along with Gus Johnstone, went into business in a mercantile in Belgrade. Both Davis and Johnstone had since sold out their interests to Rogers, perhaps in part due to an uncomfortability with Rogers, who still carried a flame for Etta. It was then unfortunate that Mr. Davis found it necessary to find work in Butte, leaving Etta to run a boardinghouse where Rogers was a tenant. Etta did not reciprocate Rogers's continual advances and in fact found them to be annoying.[38]

The night of the murder-suicide, Rogers made known his intentions to get a drink before supper. Etta attempted to persuade him not to, but Rogers bought a half pint of whiskey regardless and drank nearly all of it before sitting down to eat. Both had then gone into the sitting room, where they discussed his current lifestyle habits; after this, Etta declared she was going to the kitchen for a bath. Rogers soon followed her, and while the rest is unknown, the outcome is certain. They never left the room alive again.[39]

The hired girl had been left with the children in the sitting room, where she soon fell asleep, only aroused by the sound of something falling in the kitchen, as mentioned. Here is where the story becomes quite fascinating. When Mr. Davis arrived, he first asked the girl where his wife was, to which she answered that she did not know. Using a match, he walked about the house, peeping into the kitchen. When the hired girl went out for coal, Mr. Davis found a lamp to take a closer look in the kitchen and found his wife and Rogers in what he believed to be slumber on the floor. According to the *Standard*, "his first impulse was to kill them with an axe." He had then taken his children to Dr. McCoy's, someone they had known in North Carolina, to await the train. The paper notes he had "tears in his eyes" as he did this. Davis did not know that his wife and Rogers were, in fact, dead. He had then gone to talk to the deputy sheriff to ask for protection should Rogers become violent when he attempted to leave town with the children. Again, Mr. Davis had not the faintest idea his wife was already dead and had not been unfaithful to him as he then believed. The paper reports that it was the hired girl who first discovered that the two were dead when she went into the kitchen to start breakfast. This was near eight o'clock in the morning. She told two boarders what she had seen, and they reported it to the deputy sheriff. It was said that the "population of the town was soon following him to the scene of the tragedy."[40]

What Mr. Davis had not seen that night by lamp was now revealed by the light of day, and it was indeed a ghastly tragedy. The description of the crime scene, as reported by the *Anaconda Standard*, is as follows:

> *On the kitchen floor, with her head close to the back door, was Mrs. Davis lying on her back, with her eyes protruding in a horrible manner, the blood dyeing the floor as it had trickled in little streams from wall to wall, issuing from a gaping wound at the back of her head. At her feet lay the murderer, curled up and resting on his right side. His brains were scattered about the floor and were oozing from a large hole just in front of his right ear. Some of the spectators had stepped into the blood and carried it on their shoes all over the house, making the scene all the more ghastly.*[41]

According to the paper, the motive for the crime had been Etta's refusal to run away with Rogers. It was rumored that Rogers had made his intention to leave Belgrade "in a manner that would surprise." In this, he indeed fulfilled his wish. Etta was buried in the Bozeman cemetery on January 16 with a great procession of grievers. Rogers was buried the next day "close to her whose life he took." Etta had been just thirty-two years old. It is unknown what happened to the children or Mr. Davis following this tragedy; however, an R.L. Davis seems to have stayed in the Bozeman area till at least 1902. One must wonder, if Mr. Davis had taken an axe to the dead, would he have been considered in a plot of double murder? Would anyone have believed they had already been dead had he taken to violent action?[42]

A similar instance of extreme jealously occurred in September of the same year, 1900. This time the headline read, "Triple Tragedy." The tragedy occurred at the Rock Creek Church near the Shields River, but one of the victims had a sister in Bozeman, where his body would be interred. On September 9, Willis Howard had accompanied Flora Linn to church; when they were leaving, they were attacked by Frank Forrest. Forrest had been a suitor of Linn's but had been rejected by her in favor of Howard. As the two left the church, Forrest shot and instantly killed Howard. Linn had begun to run, but Forrest had quickly turned and taken two shots at the girl, one passing through her body and the other lodging in her heart. She did not die right away, but there was never hope for her recovery. The murderer had then taken to the brush, where he turned the gun on himself, killing himself almost instantly. It was noted that Forrest had been arrested previously for threatening the life of Howard. Howard had been thirty years old, Forrest about twenty and Linn was only sixteen. Howard is buried in Bozeman's Sunset Hills Cemetery, under an ornate headstone shaped like an old tree.[43]

The *Butte Miner* would have more of the story to share. According to this paper, Forrest had been a favored suitor of Linn's prior to the arrival of Howard. There had been talk of marriage, but when Howard arrived as a "well-to-do ranchman," Linn changed her mind on Forrest. It seems up until this point, Forrest had the "best of reputations," industrious and sober with many friends in the community. He had been asked to leave the area after being arrested for threatening Howard, and he had for a spell but had recently returned.[44]

The tragedy was even further explored in the *Anaconda Standard*'s Sunday morning edition on September 16, 1900. Nearly a full page was given to the tale alone with accompanying photographs and drawings. It seems that there was even more to the story. According to the paper, Forrest had begun courting Linn when she was just fourteen years of age. He had arrived to the area six months after the Linns had. Apparently, the fatal day had not been his only attempt at violent force. Forrest had gone to the

The headstone of Willis Howard at Sunset Hills Cemetery, Bozeman, Montana. *Author photo.*

Linn ranch with a pistol after their engagement had been broken with the intent of forcing her to marry him. She had not been home, and the gun had been taken from him by her father. He had met her on her way home and was again rejected. It was then he had vowed to kill Howard, whom he suspected as being the problem.[45]

The *Standard* blames local gossip to be the real root of the tragedy. Forrest had been assailed with jokes on his rejection, and according to the paper, "human nature, save in exceptional cases, has never been strong enough to bear this." Forrest had left town then, and his reason for returning was a mystery. It seems an unarmed Forrest had met Howard soon after his return, and the latter had found it opportune to "apply several severe and stinging epithets to him." Forrest had then begun to spread threats, which Howard had taken to heart, hence the short arrest of the former. Forrest had talked his way out of the arrest since Howard had no real proof of these accusations. Things had remained quiet for weeks until the day of the murders.[46]

That Sunday, the Linns, accompanied by Howard, had attended the little church, as had Forrest, who had slipped in the back unnoticed. As Howard and Miss Linn passed through the doorway arm in arm, Forrest had taken his chance, and within seconds both his targets had been shot. According to this paper, Forrest had run from the door into the brush, where a shot had rung out and "the body of the assassin plunged headforemost into the deepest pool of the pretty little stream." The time had been evening, and it seems that the body of Forrest was not recovered until the next morning, when both Howard and Forrest were laid side by side in front of the church door. "One form bore every trace of the manliness it had known in life, the other was wet and dripping, the hair matted, a ghastly wound in the breast, where its own hand had sent a bullet through its heart." Flora would live until Thursday morning, when she finally succumbed to her wounds.[47]

In one final paragraph, the paper sums up what may be a classic conclusion for many a story of murder: "Thus ends the story…and its tragedy. Each man had his friends, each has his defenders. Possibly one may have been too jealous, too revengeful; possibly the other was too hasty. But that they both loved and loved to desperation and death cannot be denied, and whether friend or foe the verdict of all is recorded in one brief sentence, 'It's too bad.'"[48]

Just twenty days before the Joe Fink murder, on December 2, 1915, Walter Anderson shot his wife through the window of her bedroom after smashing it

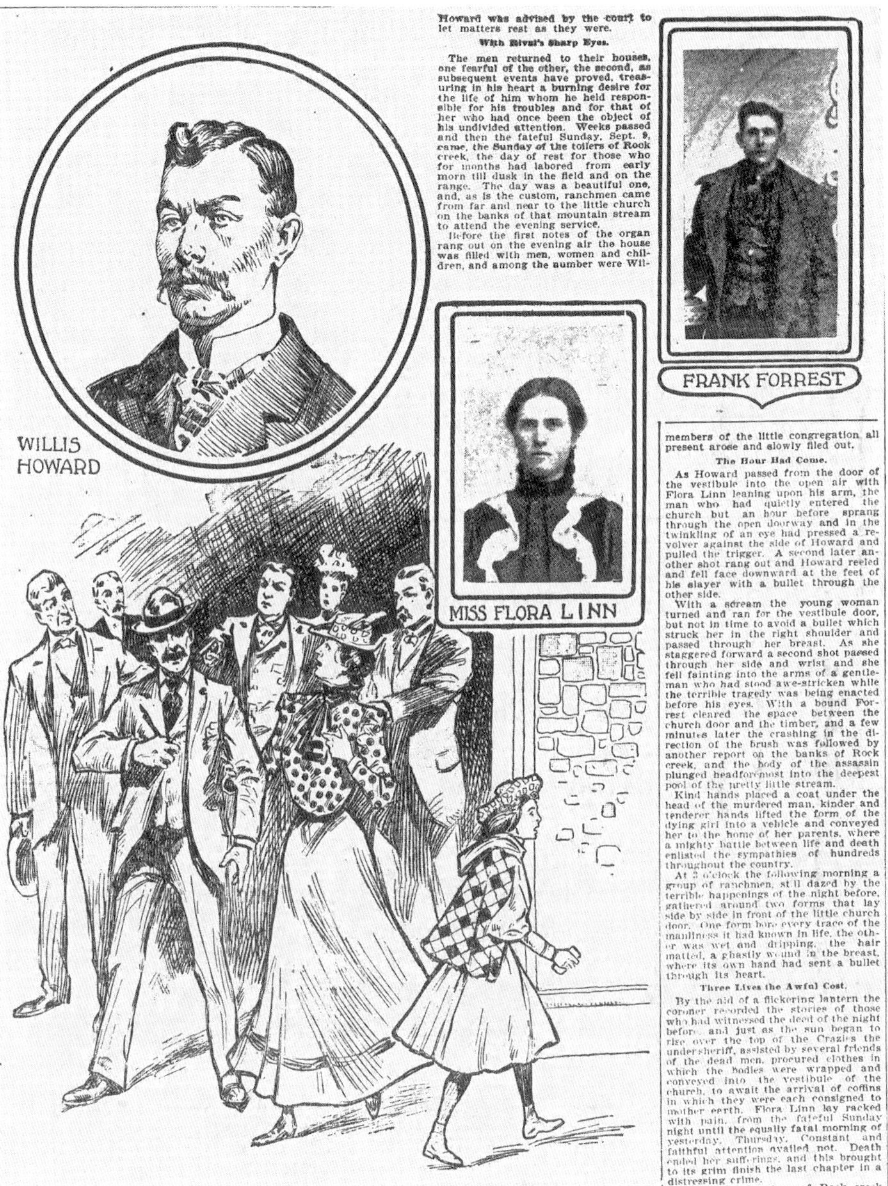

Howard was advised by the court to let matters rest as they were.

With Rival's Sharp Eyes.

The men returned to their houses, one fearful of the other, the second, as subsequent events have proved, treasuring in his heart a burning desire for the life of him whom he held responsible for his troubles and for that of her who had once been the object of his undivided attention. Weeks passed and then the fateful Sunday, Sept. 9, came, the Sunday of the toilers of Rock creek, the day of rest for those who for months had labored from early morn till dusk in the field and on the range. The day was a beautiful one, and, as is the custom, ranchmen came from far and near to the little church on the banks of that mountain stream to attend the evening service.

Before the first notes of the organ rang out on the evening air the house was filled with men, women and children, and among the number were Wil-

WILLIS HOWARD

FRANK FORREST

MISS FLORA LINN

members of the little congregation all present arose and slowly filed out.

The Hour Had Come.

As Howard passed from the door of the vestibule into the open air with Flora Linn leaning upon his arm, the man who had quietly entered the church but an hour before sprang through the open doorway and in the twinkling of an eye had pressed a revolver against the side of Howard and pulled the trigger. A second later another shot rang out and Howard reeled and fell face downward at the feet of his slayer with a bullet through the other side.

With a scream the young woman turned and ran for the vestibule door, but not in time to avoid a bullet which struck her in the right shoulder and passed through her breast. As she staggered forward a second shot passed through her side and wrist and she fell fainting into the arms of a gentleman who had stood awe-stricken while the terrible tragedy was being enacted before his eyes. With a bound Forrest cleared the space between the church door and the timber, and a few minutes later the crashing in the direction of the brush was followed by another report on the banks of Rock creek, and the body of the assassin plunged headforemost into the deepest pool of the pretty little stream.

Kind hands placed a coat under the head of the murdered man, kinder and tenderer hands lifted the form of the dying girl into a vehicle and conveyed her to the home of her parents, where a mighty battle between life and death enlisted the sympathies of hundreds throughout the country.

At 3 o'clock the following morning a group of ranchmen, still dazed by the terrible happenings of the night before, gathered around two forms that lay side by side in front of the little church door. One form bore every trace of the manliness it had known in life, the other was wet and dripping, the hair matted, a ghastly wound in the breast, where its own hand had sent a bullet through its heart.

Three Lives the Awful Cost.

By the aid of a flickering lantern the coroner recorded the stories of those who had witnessed the deed of the night before, and just as the sun began to rise over the top of the Crazies the undersheriff, assisted by several friends of the dead men, procured clothes in which the bodies were wrapped and conveyed into the vestibule of the church, to await the arrival of coffins in which they were each consigned to mother earth. Flora Linn lay racked with pain, from the fateful Sunday night until the equally fatal morning of yesterday, Thursday. Constant and faithful attention availed not. Death ended her sufferings, and this brought to its grim finish the last chapter in a distressing crime.

A drawing of Willis Howard and photographs of Miss Flora Linn and Frank Forrest featured in the *Anaconda Standard*, September 16, 1900. *Newspapers.com*.

in. It seems Mary Ellen Anderson had a man in the bedroom with her when the shots were fired, the motive behind her husband's outrage. This man was immediately taken into custody but then released on a $300 bail that bound him to appear as a witness. At the inquest, testimony was taken from the sister of Mary Ellen, Edna Marble. She had been visiting the Anderson home and had just left with a male friend, Harry Dunn, when they heard a crash and two shots. As Walter ran by, she had grabbed him, screaming, "Walter, what have you done?" to which he had replied, "I killed Mary—I shot her twice."[49]

Mary would pass away thirty hours later, making the charge of assault against Walter a far more serious charge of murder. A suit for divorce had been filed that September, and the case was pending. The trial of Walter Anderson began in February 1916, for which three key people were called to the stand: Edna Marble; A.S. Dunlap, who had been in the bedroom with Mary Ellen; and Walter himself. Edna testified to her meeting Walter on the street and his confession of the shooting. Dunlap told the jury that he had been in the bedroom when he heard the glass break. He had immediately thrown himself onto the floor and watched from there as Walter had leveled a pistol at his wife and fired twice. According to Dunlap, Walter had then told him to get up and walked him to the door with the gun pointed at him. Dr. J.F. Blair reported that either shot fired at the woman would have caused death.[50]

Walter's testimony varied from Dunlap's considerably. Walter stated that he had arrived at his house to find all the doors locked. He had heard voices in the bedroom so had peeped under the blind to see who was there. By the light coming through a cracked door, he saw his wife with Dunlap alone in the room. According to Walter, it was then "everything was dark before me and I clutched the windowsill for support." He had then broken the glass and reached under the mattress to grab a pistol he knew his wife kept there. He claimed his one thought had been to hold them in place until someone could come to see what he had seen. When Walter had looked around for his wife, Dunlap had taken the opportunity to grab his wrist. When his hand had jerked back, the gun had gone off. He said he heard moans, and wrenching his hand free from Dunlap, Walter had run to his wife, raising her in his arms as he said, "My God, Mary, were you hit?" Dunlap had left the room by this point. According to the *Anaconda Standard*, at this point in his testimony, Walter had broken down in sobs in the courtroom, stating that he would never forget that moment and that he had "loved his wife more than his life." He stated that he had not

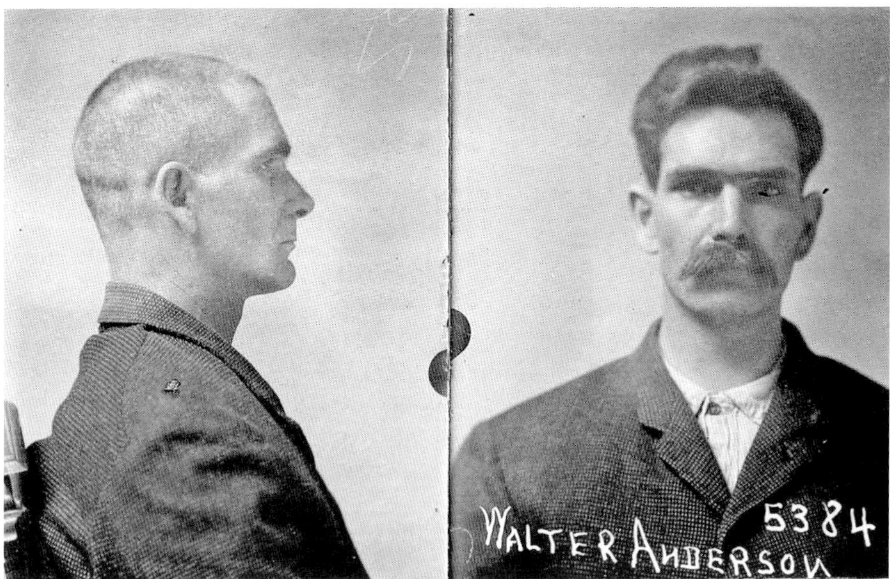

Walter Anderson, manslaughter, 1916, prison, Deer Lodge, Montana. *Montana Historical Society.*

seen his wife when the shots were fired and had not known how many there had been. He had left the house to find Dunlap, wishing him to acknowledge what had occurred at the house, but was unable to find him. He remembered meeting Edna but denied having said anything to her. He had left the pistol on the ground as his head cleared and headed for the house of Emil Zietzske to ask him to phone for the sheriff.[51]

Other witnesses called testified to Walter's recent spells of "queer" behavior, when at times his worry over the situation with his wife would overtake his mind. He would relate odd stories of impossible things that he had seen and heard at night. Even Mary Ellen herself on her deathbed would state that Walter had become insane from jealousy. The past few years of the relationship had been rocky; he had heard she had been untrue to him while he was away at a homestead. He had wanted her to join him there, but she had refused repeatedly. He stated that he had put the suspicion away from him, but seeing Dunlap with his wife that night had made everything go black for a while. In calling A.S. Dunlap's wife to the stand, it was found that her testimony differed greatly from that of her husband, although it was not reported in what ways.[52]

The jury brought back a verdict of manslaughter; Walter's sentence was fixed at ten years in the state penitentiary. The jury had brought back the verdict in an hour and twenty minutes. The defense had pleaded that Walter suffered from bouts of insanity and that one had come over him at the sight of his wife with Dunlap. Walter was taken to Deer Lodge on February 24, 1916, at the age of thirty-seven. It is unknown where he went upon his release.[53]

Chapter 3

BY PERSON OR PERSONS UNKNOWN

UNSOLVED MURDERS

Jealousy over a woman, premeditated robbery by a gang of murderers or a sudden display of uncontrollable temper in a card room brawl.
—speculated motives for the murder of Harry Walker, 1920

The unsolved murder, the puzzle that is forever unfinished, waiting to be rediscovered—this is the most fascinating type of all cases. Gallatin Valley has had its share of unsolved cases, and if one takes a look at cases with questionable outcomes like the Seth Danner trial, there may be many more that seemed closed but for which the truth was never really brought out. Someone paid the price, but did someone else get out of jail free?

On the Fourth of July 1920, a farmer fishing the Madison River about six miles above Three Forks came across the grisly scene of a body lodged in a pile of driftwood. Stripped of most of its clothing and much of its flesh, the body was difficult to identify. Collar bands still attached around the man's neck contained laundry marks, which led authorities to a laundry in Norris. The bands had remained intact due to a gunnysack that had been tied about the dead man's head with a rope before he had been put in the water. A study of the man's teeth revealed heavy gold fillings, and it was hoped these would help lead to a positive identification. Perhaps the most startling discovery, however, were two bullet holes through the man's head, clearly indicating foul play. A few days later, a coroner's jury hesitantly confirmed rumors that the body was in all probability that of Harry Walker, a ranch hand from

Madison River. *Gallatin Historical Society/Gallatin History Museum.*

Sloan Ranch who had gone missing on New Year's Eve 1919. Walker's car had been discovered in February, also in the river, but his body had not been inside. Death had been caused by the gunshot wounds fired "by persons unknown" and "at an unknown time and place." Tracing the perpetrator would prove difficult. In fact, it would prove impossible.[54]

The case would remain quiet until January 1922, when suddenly a Mrs. Laura Adams of Three Forks, proprietor of a rooming house, was arrested for the crime. The details of her arrest were at first cloudy. It seems Walker had been a boarder at Adams's house on occasion when he was in Three Forks. The complaint had been filed by the county attorney E.F. Bunker, but according to Adams, this was just a ploy by her former husband to get her out of the way since she knew something of his shady business transactions. That seemed to be the only connection, and indeed the local Bozeman paper seems to have left the case right there, as nothing more can be found about the woman's involvement or what the outcome of her situation was. A look at papers from Butte, where the murdered man, Walker, was from, and the *Anaconda Standard* detail much more of this interesting case.[55]

The *Anaconda Standard* featured a full front-page headline and three separate articles describing the case in its January 4 edition. The spread included a composite image of Mrs. Adams and the boardinghouse she ran, where it was believed Walker had been killed. According to the paper, three motives had been proposed for Walker's murder: "jealousy over a woman, premeditated robbery by a gang of murderers or a sudden display of uncontrollable temper in a card room brawl." Each motive was then elaborated on. It seems rumored that Adams (a divorcée of between two and four men) had recently become the fiancée of Walker, which had made certain men jealous. The second, robbery, was indicated by several people who believed Walker had between $1,500 and $2,000, which he had shown in town on the night of the twenty-sixth. The third motive was made possible by a belief that Walker had been playing cards at the Adams boardinghouse on the night in question. It was only very briefly mentioned that Adams, his possible fiancée, may have killed Walker herself at her establishment. A motive for this last possibility was established by a William Miller, a manservant of the boardinghouse; however, his story was not shared in the paper. It does seem like it was on his word that Adams had found herself arrested for first-degree murder. However, it was also believed that Walker had not been to the hotel that night and that Adams had been ill in bed for days before and after Walker's disappearance. If this is true, then the murder having been committed by Adams or as the result of a rough card game are both an impossibility, which leaves jealousy and robbery as the two possible motives.[56]

However, the *Augusta News* of Augusta, Montana, seemed to know more about Adams's possible motive and involvement. In this telling of events, it was believed that robbery had indeed been the motive. According to this story, Walker had been celebrating at a New Year's Eve party at the Adams hotel when the latter and her fellow men realized the amount of money Walker had on his person. They had murdered him in the house and then done away with the body and his car. This seems to be the reason why Adams was arrested and perhaps was a better telling than the story for which William Miller was being held as a witness. In Miller's telling of this story, Mrs. Adams had claimed Walker died by suicide, as he had left a note behind at the Sloan Ranch stating he was going away and that all his money was to pay his debts. However, it seems unlikely Walker put a gunnysack full of rocks over his head after he was dead.[57]

For ten months following the discovery of Walker's body, detectives had been working as undercover ranch hands among the men suspected of

Name Laura Adams

No. Finger Print Class.

Laura Adams, suspicion of murder, 1922, Gallatin County jail. *Gallatin Historical Society/ Gallatin History Museum.*

knowing something about the case. The culmination of their work had been the arrest of Adams, although still, the motive and means by which she would have committed the murder were unclear to the public. Several men were under surveillance, including two men who had visited the Sloan Ranch that night and asked him to accompany them to town. In this latter investigation, it was proposed that the two men had picked up Walker and a rifle at the ranch. A rifle belonging to Sloan was indeed missing. On the way to Three Forks, the man riding in the back seat had shot Walker twice while the other drove. The car was driven over a one-hundred-foot embankment into the Madison and a gunnysack full of rocks had been tied about the dead man's head to keep him securely at the bottom of the river. The motive could have been either jealousy, as one of the men had shown signs, or robbery of the large amount of money Walker had. However plausible this scenario is, it was Mrs. Adams who was under arrest, not either of these men indicated.[58]

This confusing case became even more convoluted when the *Anaconda Standard* published an article titled "Depicts Murder Scene as Given Her by Occult," which ran parallel to the one on possible motives. A correspondent of the *Standard* was on the scene at the Gallatin County jail, where Adams, in a large room, sat with an arm around both of her children proclaiming her innocence and describing the murder as told to her by a spirit medium from Willow Creek. According to Adams, the male medium, referred to only as Moore, saw

> *a high bank and said that he could see Walker approaching in his car…it was just before sundown when he* [Walker] *recognized two men fishing on a flat below. He thought he might get a drink with them. With one of the men Walker had previously had some kind of misunderstanding…when Walker approached, he was attacked…and would have been able to defend himself ably enough had not one of them seized a gun and fired. The body was then done away with under a pile of brush in the river and the car run over the bank. One of the assailants was injured and was carried to a ranch house not far away.*

Adams was able to identify the two men the medium had seen as well as the one who had pulled the trigger. According to Adams, she claimed she had "been arrested and charged with murder because the booze runners are trying to put me out of the way—just as they got rid of Walker." She had indeed intended to marry Walker but had feared for her life if they had. It seems Adams had been married four times previously: the first had been annulled due to her husband already being married, her second husband was shot and killed while standing beside her at their home in Texas and the third and fourth she had divorced, the last being a prominent rancher near Three Forks.

Despite all these different theories, it seems the crime could not be pinned on Adams or any of her companions. She would be released in March 1922 and dismissed of all charges. Adams would continue to be of interest to the *Butte Miner*, which would print her corrections to facts that had been printed in various newspapers during the case. According to Adams, her second husband had in fact been killed at his store while she had been in the back, and she had used up nearly every cent of his estate trying to track down his killer, per her husband's request. She stated that she had never been apart from her two children from her third marriage until she had been arrested and that she had never been in the company of Walker alone. She claimed to have only been near him twice and her children had been with her both times. According to Adams, "This has been my stormy career. I was the victim of blackmail and charged with a crime I had nothing whatever to do with. Since my arrest I have been constantly under a physician's care." This bold statement seems highly at

WHERE BUTTE MAN MAY HAVE BEEN MURDERED

The Dempsey lodging house at Three Forks run by Mrs. Laura Adams, who is held on the charge of being concerned in the murder of Harry L. Walker two years ago. It is one of the theories of the authorities that Walker may have been killed in this house and his body taken in his own automobile to the point where the car was driven into the river from a high embankment. Inset is Mrs. Adams.

Laura Adams and the Dempsey Lodging House in Three Forks, where Harry Walker may have been murdered. Adams later claimed this photo was not of her. *From the* Anaconda Standard, *January 4, 1922, Newspapers.com.*

odds with many parts of the case; if she had not been alone with Walker ever, how then was it assumed they were to be married, and why did she once say she feared for their lives should they be married? Furthermore, why did she see a medium about the case prior to her arrest if she had nothing to do with Walker and his murder?[59]

The case would dissolve into nothing following Adams's release until the summer of 1923, when Seth Orrin Danner was arrested for the murder of Florence and John Sprouse. While at the Gallatin County jail, Danner mentioned that he knew someone who knew something of the Walker case but that the person did not live about there anymore. This brief mention led to a reexamination of the case, to the point that Seth Danner himself was alleged to have committed the crime. After all, his supposed victim, John Sprouse, had also been discovered with a gunnysack tied over his head. Seth Danner likely had been in South Dakota at the time of Walker's death, making his involvement impossible. The rumors quickly quieted in light of the dramatic Danner case and his eventual execution (see chapter 7).

The death of Harry Walker remains an unsolved murder to this day. Laura Adams's own murder in 1941 would end differently. Her killer would be sent to prison for life (see chapter 4).

The unsolved cases detailed in this chapter are just a sample of those in Gallatin County, where, in fact, a string of unsolved murders dot the local landscape: a skeleton washed up on a sandbar of the Madison River, much like that of Harry Walker; remains found near railroad tracks; men discovered next to the roads at Chestnut and Manhattan; bodies found in the woods about Central Park—all unknown persons, all unsolved to this day. Then there are those who are named: Mrs. McCoy's sister, found shot in the head on the stairs of a house in Belgrade; Boyd Flemming, found dead in a cabin up Sixteen Mile Creek; and Robert McClelland, shot through the window of a Manhattan house. Those named and unnamed are now just a note in a file of murders at the Gallatin History Museum and even the dates lost to time.

Chapter 4

TO HAVE AND HAVE NOT

MOTIVE, ROBBERY

Judge, I am as innocent of the crime as you are.
—Lucy Black, second-degree murder, 1901

Jealousy of what others have has long been a motive for crime. Sometimes it results in a clean robbery, someone gets away taking what wasn't theirs, but no one is physically hurt. Sometimes the robbery goes wrong, the perpetrator gets caught or the only witness is sacrificed. And sometimes murder is the only way to get at what one wants. The reward outweighs the crime, just as long as one doesn't get caught.

The front page of the October 12, 1901 *Avant Courier* blared the headline "Death by Poison!" It was apparent immediately that this death had been no accident. According to the subheading, this was the second time that John H. Black, a prominent citizen of Salesville, had been poisoned, but this time, the result had been fatal. The headline alone would have been enough to spark anyone's interest in the case, as most murders in the area were the result of gunshot or knife wounds. However, the case grew even more fascinating in the last paragraph of the article, where the paper broke the news that the wife of Mr. Black, Lucy, and a hired man, Fred Auger, had been arrested on suspicion.[60]

It seems the first attempt at poisoning had been made in August over a dinner of ham. Mr. and Mrs. Black and Ira DeLong (also of Salesville) had eaten together at Mrs. Black's homestead near Camp Creek. At the time, it had been believed that the ham had been poisoned, as it had "been left in the unoccupied house for some time." It is unclear if it was believed the ham had been poisoned intentionally while left alone or if it had simply gone bad due to being left out. Only Mr. Black and DeLong were taken ill on this occasion, but both had recovered.[61]

On Friday, October 4, the same party had returned to the homestead, this time having oxtail soup, which they had brought with them. Again Mr. Black and DeLong were taken ill. DeLong, while badly off, recovered; Mr. Black, however, was brought to Bozeman for medical treatment after vomiting for days. The couple had stayed at the Central Beer Hall lodging house while in town. Dr. C.M. Chambliss had prescribed John to eat peptonized beef but was surprised when he checked on him on Sunday to find he had eaten a quantity of peaches and seemed to be doing just fine. He was well enough to return home; however, Lucy soon returned to town to ask for something to help quiet her husband, who was still unwell and had been walking about outside in only his nightshirt, out of his mind, according to Lucy. Upon a visit from Dr. Chambliss to the ranch on Tuesday, Black was found to be quite ill. The doctor believed John should be moved back to Bozeman, but Lucy resisted, saying they had enough money to pay for the doctor's visits. The next day, Lucy returned to ask the doctor to visit on Thursday, which he did promptly. Upon his arrival, Lucy had been eating breakfast with Fred Auger and had asked the doctor to make her husband's will. The doctor had not answered but instead had gone to see John, whom he found suffering from morphine and very ill. Another hired hand, Andy Anderson, had been called for to give John a bath and keep him awake and alert while the doctor drove to Alex Black's (John's brother) house. He told Alex that he firmly believed John was being poisoned. Together they had gone back to see John and found that Lucy had thrown Andy out of John's room. Lucy vehemently protested them taking John to Bozeman. However, she eventually lost control of the situation when police and a deputy sheriff were called to watch John's room at the infirmary, where he died on Thursday night. It was clear that he had indeed been poisoned and that the poison had gone through his whole system, making it impossible to supply an antidote. There was nothing the doctor could have done to save him. The next day, Friday, Coroner Finlay was working to understand the form of poison that had killed Black.[62]

The next week, on October 19, it was announced that Coroner Finlay had scientifically found poison in Black's system. The poison(s) employed would not be revealed until the trial, but it was enough for the coroner's jury to declare Black's death had been caused by poison administered by Lucy Black, his wife. Lucy was quickly arraigned before Judge McPherson and was, according to the *Avant Courier*, "as dumb as the proverbial oyster, absolutely refusing to answer any question put to her by the court, even in monosyllables." She was charged with murder. Fred Auger remained in custody under the suspicion of having aided Lucy in the poisoning. There is no record in the jail ledgers of his release, but it seems when it came time for the trial, he was no longer implicated in the ordeal and must have been given his freedom.[63]

The character of Black, for those who did not know the man, was detailed in this half obituary, half detective story article. John Black was buried on the afternoon of October 17, exactly a week following his death. It was noted that John had been a large, healthy person, full of energy until stricken by this unexpected malady. He was born in Missouri on October 2, 1847, coming to Montana in 1875 and to Gallatin County in 1880. He had maintained a prosperous farm in Salesville, doing well enough to become known as a moneylender. According to the paper, "nothing was apparently too good for his friends, while he had but little if any kind of consideration for his enemies. In these respects, there was a good deal of human nature mixed up in his composition." John had been fifty-four years old upon his death. He had been married at a young age and had two grown children living back east who were expected to arrive in Bozeman at some point. John and his first wife, Alice Daems, had divorced in 1883. Lucy Kirkpatrick had been his second wife, and it was believed in this article that she had not only tried to poison him the two times listed previously but had indeed slowly been poisoning him over the two years they had been together.[64]

The preliminary hearing, set for Friday October 25, did not go further than the testimony of Dr. Chambliss, who had attended to John in his infirmary. The hearing was then postponed due to the serious illness of the prosecuting attorney's father.[65] The hearing would finally finish on October 31, which kept Lucy Black at the county jail to be held without bail until her trial. While the trial had been expected to begin that November, there had not been time between the preliminary hearing and the start of the court term for the prosecuting attorney to put together the case. On November 30, 1901, it was announced that the trial of Lucy Black would begin in February 1902, prosecuting county attorney George Pease having formally filed the charge against her. The means of poisoning were now revealed to be morphine, opium and arsenic.[66]

John Black. *From the* Anaconda Standard, *February 2, 1902, Newspapers.com.*

Interestingly, in early January, it was noted that an application had been submitted asking the court to show cause why the homestead of the late John Black had not been made for the use of his surviving wife. Little had been discussed about Lucy Black and her history up to this point, as so much of the media had been focused on John, his life and his untimely death. Lucy was born in 1863 in Kentucky, her maiden name being Ray. She had married a John Kirkpatrick from whom she had been divorced in 1900. She had one child with John Kirkpatrick, Lula, who was born in 1882. Lula had been married in 1898 to Richard Afflack in Bozeman. Lula, interestingly, is not mentioned in any of the articles related to the trial and case, although she seems to have been living in the area at the time. According to the *Avant Courier*, Lucy had begun working for John Black as a housekeeper in May 1900, and by October of the same year, they were married in Livingston.[67]

The trial started on February 3, with the first day used up in picking the jury. The following day, Hartman and Hartman appeared as attorneys for the state, which had come as a surprise to the defending attorneys, as they had not been listed as such. All objections, however, were overruled, and Mr. Hartman was allowed to proceed in his opening statements to the jury followed by a short statement by L.A. Luce on behalf of the defendant. Luce's statement was simple: if the prosecution could not deliver on all of the facts it said it was going to prove, then a verdict of not guilty must be returned.[68]

The first witness called was Alex Black, brother of the deceased, John Black. Alex had not been acquainted with his brother's estate and financial affairs until called to be the administrator after his death. According to Alex, John's estate was appraised at $30,000. Alex had called on his brother on October 8, when John had been ill, and again on the tenth, when he had died. He testified to believing that his brother had died from "knock-out drops." The doctor was then called on to discuss the various effects of drugs like opium, morphine and the like and how he had tried to combat the effects of these drugs in John Black when he had been brought to the infirmary. During cross-examination of the doctor, "the fur began to fly." Lucy was well informed on drugs and their effects and led the doctor on a pretty good chase of different theories.[69]

Two different witnesses were called to testify to capsules Mrs. Black had picked up at the Osborn Drug Company in October 1901; however, in both instances, the substance of the capsules could not be identified, and neither witness was cross-examined. This was followed by examinations of those who had performed the autopsy and prepared the body of John Black for burial.[70]

A Mark White was called to the stand to recall seeing Ira DeLong on October 4 along Shed's Bridge, where DeLong had asked White to get him something to stop the pain he was in. DeLong had been visibly quite ill. White had gotten him essence of peppermint, which seemed to have eased the pain of cramps he had in his stomach. To relate the strange illnesses of DeLong and John Black, Sheriff Fowler was called to describe the arrest of

Lucy Black at the Central Beer Hall lodging house on October 10 and the contents of a valise found with her person. Deputy Sheriff David Tudor had found similar bottles at the ranch that same day. The contents of these bottles were not revealed until the third day of the trial, when they were all discussed by Dr. Traphagen as to their chemical content. However, the paper did not reveal what the doctor had to say about them. The leftover can from the oxtail soup had been found in the yard of the homestead and was introduced as evidence. The *Avant Courier* noted, "The store of drugs and secondhand goods put in evidence still keeps increasing and it looks as though a special deputy would soon be needed to handle it." The paper also posited that the physician's portion of testimony had been over many of the jurors' heads, with so many unpronounceable names it was hard to tell if the doctor had been trying to explain things to the jury or just show off his knowledge. Most of their testimony contradicted one another on the type of poison used, which led to cloudy evidence in the eyes of the jury.[71]

The local public had taken quite an interest in the case, particularly the ladies, who kept the courtroom filled the whole time. According to the paper, Lucy Black, while self-possessed and interested in the proceedings, was starting to show the effects of the ordeal she was going through, which many believed to be of life or death. It was not until Saturday morning, February 8, that a verdict was returned. To the surprise of many, the verdict was guilty on a count of manslaughter. It seems, however, the jury had not found the evidence sufficient to charge Lucy with first-degree murder. After much deliberation (thirteen hours), the jury was allowed to bring in the lesser charge of manslaughter. The charge was for having administered ten grains of arsenic, twenty grains of opium and twenty grains of morphine to John Black. The defense stated that the drugs had been administered by Lucy with the hope of "producing temporary effect so as to enable Mrs. Black to influence her husband in his making a will to suit her wishes but not with intent to commit murder."[72]

Lucy Black. *From the* Butte Daily Post, *February 13, 1902, Newspapers.com.*

Local residents had been mostly set against Lucy from the start; there had even been talk of a possible lynching. A good portion of the negativity against Lucy had come from women, many of whom had been gossiping about an "unsavory" reputation and past, although it was never stated in print what that past was. When read the verdict and punishment, Lucy had seemed to cheer up considerably; it seems she too had been thinking her sentence would be dire. In total, the case had taken six days in a courtroom and had cost the county $2,000. On Saturday, February 15, Lucy was officially sentenced by Judge Holloway to Deer Lodge State Prison for a term of ten years. According to the *Avant Courier*, "the Judge told her that her sex prevented a verdict of murder in the first degree." When she had been asked if she had anything to say, she stated, "Judge, I am as innocent of the crime as you are." While she seemed relieved at her light sentencing, her attorneys did attempt to file a motion in arrest of judgment, but it was overruled. It was believed that would be the last of the Black "tragedy."[73]

The case had been of interest throughout Montana with special dispatches sent to local town papers, including the *Anaconda Standard*, which took a keen interest in the case, dramatizing the murder and trial in words and imagery not seen in the local Bozeman paper. There were also new details that added color to the story. For example, on the arrest of Lucy, the *Standard* detailed that she had been found in bed and that when she was told to consider herself under arrest, she had stated that she had expected it. She later said it was the "work of her enemies; that she had downed them once and would do so again." When the sheriff had gone through Lucy's valise, she had asked for a box that had morphine in it; when that request was refused, she had asked for a glass of whiskey. The paper further noted that Lucy was "not at all bad looking," which some came to speculate on later, after her trial and sentencing.[74]

On February 14, 1902, the *Anaconda Standard* published an article titled "An Illogical Verdict" in which the jury of the Black case was chastised for having brought back such a light charge as manslaughter. According to the paper, "someone suggested not long ago that it would be better to arrange criminal trials so that female defendants would be tried by female juries in order that the element of sexual attraction might be eliminated. It was argued that when a woman was on trial before a jury composed entirely of men their natural instinct to shield and protect all of her sex worked to defeat the ends of justice. The case of Mrs. Lucy S. Black seems to bear out this theory." The paper goes on to say that it was clear there were only two options for the jury since the poison that killed John Black was so premeditatedly given: guilty of murder in the first or not guilty at all. It was believed by the author that the jury of men had not wanted Lucy to suffer but also had not wanted to let her escape punishment entirely. As the author notes, the flaw was in the system of law rather than the jurors, as all men would be the same, shrinking from "the thought of sending a woman to the gallows, though she be as guilty as a Borgia." The death penalty was the only punishment related to first-degree murder at that time, leaving the jurors looking for a variant charge to avoid the fate of death for Lucy.[75]

Perhaps the best imagery to come out of any murder trial in Bozeman was printed in the *Anaconda Standard*. In a full-page section titled "Bozeman's Murder Case," the main characters in the case as well as the courthouse where the trial occurred all were pictured under the arms of a hooded figure of justice with a scale in one hand and a sword in the other accompanied by the devil, poison bottles, a graveyard and even some bats. Coincidentally or not, the hooded figure looks a lot like Lucy Black herself. Lucy would serve a reduced sentence of six years, being released in May 1908, after which her story has been lost to time.

In September 1905, Jack Kennan was killed "within feet of twenty men," according to breaking headlines in Bozeman's *Republican Courier*. It was a stabbing incident committed outside a saloon in Manhattan around eleven thirty at night. With the first news of the crime came the news that Frank Purcell and Tom Shannon had been arrested on suspicion. The murder came following an evening of raucous behavior on the part of Jack Kennan, who had been drinking heavily at various saloons in the town. He had been ordered out of one where he had apparently abused the patrons. Kennan had arrived at George Herndon's place, where he attempted to start a fight with Robert Speidleberg, with whom he'd had a drink, stating that he would "knock his head off." The former stated that he would "put the gloves on with him," but Kennan declined. It was about this time that Frank Purcell, who had been sitting across the room, came over and punched Kennan, knocking him to his knees. As Kennan had attempted to rise, Purcell and Shannon had pushed him out the screen door and onto the sidewalk. Those inside would testify to hearing blows thrown outside the saloon.[76]

The next thing everyone saw was Shannon returning and, a few seconds later, Purcell, who was dragging Kennan's body and calling for someone to get a doctor because Kennan had "cut himself." George Herndon testified to having seen Shannon wash his bloody hands in a washbowl upon reentering, and another witness stated that Shannon had a knife in his hand. Upon investigation the next morning, authorities discovered pools of blood on the sidewalk, and sixty feet from the saloon, signs of a struggle and the marks of a man being dragged were evident. It was noted by the

PAGES 17 TO 28

The Anaconda Standard.

EDITORIAL SECTION

ANACONDA, MONTANA, SUNDAY, FEBRUARY 2, 1902.

Bozeman's Murder Case

BOZEMAN, Feb. 1.—The famous Black poisoning case will come up for trial Monday morning. This case is one of the most interesting as well as mysterious that has ever been up for trial in Gallatin county district court, or for that matter in the state of Montana.

So far as can be ascertained there was no motive for the crime and it is hard to tell why, if it is true, Mrs. Lucy S. Black should have taken her husband's life and in taking it should have used the means she did. She claims she is innocent of the crime and in the eyes of the law she is until convicted. The question that is puzzling the public is "Was John H. Black poisoned, and if Mrs. Black did not poison him, who did?

The information reads substantially as follows: "On the 25th day of November, 1901, Lucy S. Black is accused by the county attorney of the county of Gallatin of the crime of murder, the said Lucy S. Black on the 4th day of October, 1901, and on each day from then till the including 10th day of October, 1901, making an assault in and upon John H. Black and did then and there during the times aforesaid unlawfully, feloniously and of her deliberately, premeditatedly malice aforethought administer to and cause to be administered to and taken by the said John H. Black into his stomach and body so as to injure the life of said John H. Black certain dangerous, unwholesome, pernicious, destructive and noxious poisons in deadly quantities to-wit, 10 grains of the deadly poison called arsenic and 20 grains of the deadly poison called opium and 20 grains of the deadly poison called morphine, etc., and the taking of the said deadly poisons aforesaid into the stomach and body of said John H. Black as aforesaid, he the said John H. Black became, then and there during the times aforesaid mortally sick and distempered in his body and by reason of such mortal sickness and distemper did continually languish until on the 10th day of October, 1901, etc."

Story of the Crime.

Some time in July or August John H. Black, his wife, Lucy S. Black, and Ira DeLong went up to a homestead owned by Mrs. Black in the vicinity of Camp creek, some distance west of Salesville. After eating a meal prepared by Mrs. Black her husband and Ira DeLong were taken with severe vomiting but recovered after a few days. At that time it was believed some of John Black's enemies had placed strychnine in the ham which formed part of the meal and which had been in the cabin on the homestead for some time.

On Friday, Oct. 10, the same trio made another visit to the same place, but this time they took their dinner along with them and among other things had a can of ox tail soup which formed the principal feature of the meal prepared on that day by Mrs. Black. After eating somewhat heartily of the soup and other items which formed the rather rough menu, the two men again became very sick and vomited violently. On neither occasion was Mrs. Black afflicted to any marked degree by the malady or poison which threatened at that time to end the lives of the two men.

After a short time Mr. and Mrs. Black drove home to their ranch just a little north of Salesville, Mr. Black vomiting all the way home, while Ira DeLong followed them on horseback and arrived at the ranch some time after they did. The next day both men were still suffering, but John Black was apparently quite ill. Accordingly Mr. and Mrs. Black came to Bozeman Saturday Oct. 5, and called on Dr. Chambliss to consult him with reference to the illness of Mr. Black. During the consultation John Black stated he thought he had eaten something that had disagreed with him, as he was still vomiting, and after describing his symptoms to the doctor he was prescribed some peptonized beef and other simple remedies. The next morning, Sunday, Oct. 6, Dr. Chambliss called on Black, who was staying in the Central Beer hall lodging house, and was surprised to find he had eaten a number of peaches and seemed to be nearly well. That afternoon Black and his wife went to their ranch near Salesville.

Monday evening Mrs. Black called at the doctor's office on Main street and stated that her husband was still unwell and that he had been walking around outdoors with only his night-shirt on and he seemed to be out of his head, and asked the doctor for something to quiet him. Some simple medicine was given and the next day, Tuesday, Dr. Chambliss drove out to Salesville and found his patient quite sick and wanted him brought to town, but Mrs. Black said they had plenty of money and they were able to pay for the visits he made to the ranch.

Some Queer Circumstances.

Wednesday Mrs. Black was again a caller at Dr. Chambliss' office and it was arranged he should make a professional visit the next day. The doctor kept his promise. He arrived at the Black ranch about 11 o'clock and found Mrs. Black and the hired man, Fred Ainger, eating their breakfast. While the doctor was removing his coat Mrs. Black asked him to make her husband's will, and instead of replying he went on into the sick room. He found Black apparently suffering from morphine and in a very bad condition. As quickly as possible he gave him some antidotes, slapped him and tried to rouse him out of his sleep, and after working with him for some time he sent out for Andy Anderson, another hired man. While Mrs. Black demurred somewhat to the request of Dr. Chambliss, Anderson was finally sent for. When he arrived the doctor told him to give Black a bath and keep him awake, but not to give him anything to drink. The doctor, after making some excuses, drove to the ranch of A. H. Black, who resided close by, and explained to him that he believed John Black was being poisoned. A. H., or Alex Black, as he is more commonly known, and Dr. Chambliss returned to the John Black ranch. In the meantime Anderson had been told to get out of the sick chamber and was outside of the house when the doctor returned.

After the objections of Mrs. Black had been overcome it was agreed to remove John Black to town, and it was suggested he be taken to either of the two hospitals. John Black was then placed in a wagon and accompanied by Ainger and Mrs. Black was brought to Bozeman, but instead of being removed to a hospital he was taken to the Central Beer hall lodging house and Dr. Safeley sent for. When Dr. Safeley arrived he found the sick man was evidently suffering from the effects of poison of some character, and after using remedies he ordered Black taken to Chambliss' infirmary. To enforce the order he called in some of the police and the deputy sheriff. The sick man was taken to the infirmary about 7.15 Thursday evening. Immediately after his ar-

(Continued on Page Nineteen.)

Full page of the *Anaconda Standard* featuring "Bozeman's Murder Case," February 2, 1902. *Newspapers.com*.

PUBLICAN-C

GALLATIN COUNTY, MONTANA FRIDAY SEPT 15, 1905.

ANOTHER MURDER

Jack Kennan Killed Within a Few Feet of Twenty Men.

TWO CHARGED WITH THE CRIME

For Some Unknown Cause a Man is Murdered in Cold Blood. All Connected With the Crime Had Been Drinking.

Another murder, committed in Manhattan, was added to Gallatin county's list of crimes Tuesday night. Jack Kennan, a lumberjack, thresherman, jack-of-all-trades, was stabbed at a point over the right clavical and the sub-clavian

committed close to the saloon. There were three or four pools of blood on the little sidewalk or platform just outside the door. However, about sixty feet north east from the saloon, out in the dusty road or street, were some

Left: Headlines from the *Republican-Courier*, September 15, 1905, on the Jack Kennan murder. *Gallatin Historical Society/Gallatin History Museum.*

Below: Manhattan saloon much like the one Kennan was murdered near. *Gallatin Historical Society/Gallatin History Museum.*

paper that Kennan was a small man, only about 150 pounds, while Purcell was a heavily built man, weighing about 200 pounds. Interestingly, it was stated that Shannon was a "rather small fellow and does not look like a murderer." It seems Speidleberg was also taken to the county jail and held as a witness. The knife that supposedly did the deed was found in Purcell's pocket. Kennan had died within minutes of receiving the wound, for the knife had entered above his right clavicle and cut an artery. Both Purcell and Shannon would state that Kennan had cut himself.[77]

It seems there was another witness held at the jail pending the trial of Purcell and Shannon, a William Buckley. On October 2, it was announced that the man had been taken to the Warm Springs insane asylum. According to a dispatch to the *Butte Miner* from Bozeman, he had been held with his consent but had brooded over the murder "until his mind lost its balance." When his mental state was noticed, he was urged to leave the jail; however, he was terrified of being poisoned if he did and refused to leave. His refusal soon led to violence, and local doctors thought it best he spend some time at Warm Springs to recover his senses.[78]

The trial of Frank Purcell would take place in October, just one month following the murder. The state called nine witnesses, one of them being Shannon, who was freed that morning from any murder charges. When Purcell was put on the stand and cross-examined, he was addressed as Dick Frame, a man who had been tried for highway robbery in Wyoming earlier that year. It seems Purcell and Frame were one and the same. The trial lasted only a few days, with a verdict coming in after just five hours of deliberation. Purcell was found guilty of murder in the second degree. As punishment, Judge Stewart sentenced Purcell to life at the state penitentiary with hard labor.[79]

On September 20, 1934, war veteran William Kelly was found dead along Keggy Lane, a short road that led off Sourdough and was commonly referred to as Lover's Lane. The back of his head had been nearly blown off by a shotgun charge at close range. Evidence suggested that the man had fallen face forward when shot and then had been rolled onto his back, in which position the killer had turned out his pockets. Almost immediately, several men were brought in for questioning, including Clarence Arnold, Earl and William Pierce, Lee Ping (a repeat visitor at the jail) and James Deskin. All but Deskin were released from custody. His car was also being held for inspection, believed by authorities to be the car in which "Kelly had been taken for a ride." Kelly had only just arrived to the area on the invite of Clarence Arnold, who had known Kelly at a veteran's hospital at Fort Harrison. Kelly had been forty-five years old.[80]

Two days later, a coroner's jury arrived at a verdict: "that the said William Kelly was shot and killed by an unknown person or persons." It was not until Monday that Deskin was charged with the murder. Apparently, evidence had arisen to give weight to a prosecution of Deskin, although he still chose to plead not guilty. November 21 was the first day of the Deskin trial. Earlier in the week, Dan Holland had been found guilty and sentenced to life imprisonment for the killing of Frank Sparlin (see chapter 1). The first day of the trial was taken up by jury selection, followed by prosecuting attorney Fred Lay's opening statements. According to Lay, the prosecution was going to show how on the day of the murder Deskin, Kelly, Arnold, Pierce and Ping had all been playing cards and drinking at Arnold's shack in Bozeman when Kelly had slapped Deskin's face after the latter had called him a "foul name" three times. The prosecution was going to prove how this altercation, though seemingly resolved at the time, had lingered in the mind of Deskin. How later that day, when Deskin, Arnold and Kelly went out to hunt prairie chickens, Deskin's rage had taken a physical shape. It was believed that when Kelly had asked Deskin to stop the car for a few minutes, most likely as a rest stop, the fatal act had occurred.[81]

Witnesses had then been called to testify, the first being Robert Phillips, who had been the first to discover the body of Kelly with three companions on the night of the murder. Police officers Anderson and Isbell were called to corroborate what happened following the discovery. The following day, witnesses continued to be called; in total, there would be twenty-eight for the prosecution and nine for the defense.[82]

Deskin would take the stand in his own defense. According to the accused, he had never had an altercation with Kelly and had not gone hunting with Arnold and Kelly. In fact, he claimed that Arnold had wanted Deskin to hock his shotgun to get funds for their bootlegging operations. Mrs. Deskin had apparently talked him out of that idea, and the gun had been taken to Guy Griffen for safekeeping. Pierce, Arnold and Deskin had taken Mrs. Deskin home from grocery shopping in the car when they had an altercation. Bizarrely, Arnold supposedly took the car away on a signal from Deskin, following which the couple had made peace. Dinner had been made, their children called for and the night spent peacefully at home until the next morning, when law enforcement had arrived and made the arrest. The defense argued that this was "one of those perfect crimes you read about" where Deskin had been set up to take the fall. According to the defense, Deskin had been nowhere near the scene of the crime, and his car and an old empty shell from his shotgun had been used to frame him. According to Mrs. Deskin, the empty shells had been in the car because their son liked to play with them. Witnesses were called to testify on Deskin's behalf, while others were called to support the theory that a slap had turned sour.[83]

Evidence such as clothing, footprints, Deskin's shotgun and photographs of the dead man were introduced. A bacteriologist from Montana State College was put on the stand to testify that blood found on the shoes of Arnold and Deskin and in the Deskin car was human blood. The embalmer, Charles Raper of Dokken Funeral Home, testified to his examination of the body that night and the estimation of time of death. The most damaging testimony, however, was that of Arnold, who told his story of the car ride to hunt prairie chickens, the stop alongside the road and the shock when Deskin took aim and fired his shotgun into the back of Kelly's head. Arnold stated he exclaimed, "My God, Deskin, why did you do that?" to which Deskin had replied that "no man could slap his face and get away with it," or, as other papers would report, "No —— can slap me and get away with it." He had forced Arnold to roll the body over out of the way of the car and then threatened him never to tell what had happened. The defense attempted to discredit Arnold by cross-examination of other witnesses, one of whom stated that Arnold had said during the drinking party that "he wished Kelly would pass out so they could roll him."[84]

The case drew to a close on the evening of the twenty-fourth, and the jury was out for twelve and a half hours, until 10:00 a.m. on Sunday morning, when they returned a verdict of guilty on the count of first-degree murder. Like Holland, Deskin would receive a sentence of life imprisonment that morning. The prosecution had asked for the death penalty; however, it seems even on a first-degree murder charge, Deskin managed to escape that fate. According to reports, Deskin was said to have smiled "slightly to his guard" and said simply, "Let's go" after being given his sentencing.

On August 17, 1941, it was announced that Mrs. Laura Adams was missing. It had been twenty-two years since Harry Walker had gone missing and then turned up dead, a crime in which Adams had been implicated. On the night of August 14, Adams (then age sixty) had left her lodging house with a man, telling people she had planned to drive twelve miles to a ranch along the Madison River and that she planned to return right away. It was reported that the couple had gotten gas along the way, attended by Harold

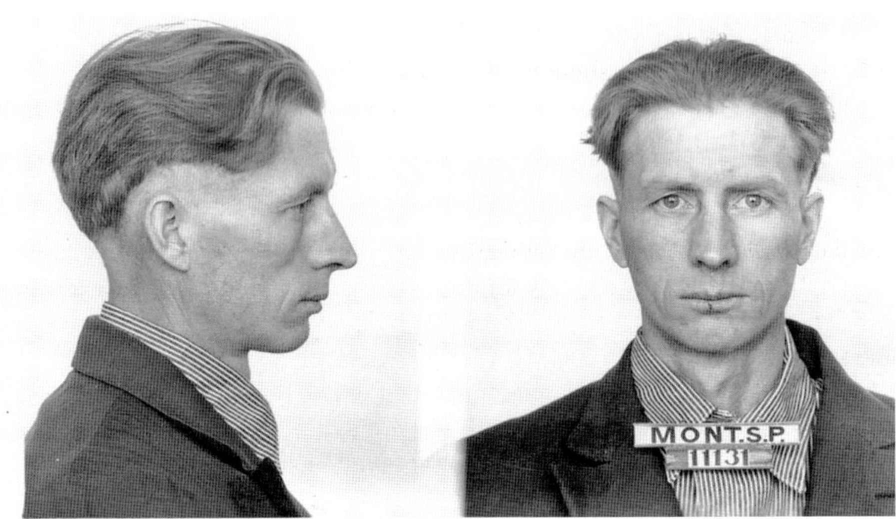

James Deskin, first-degree murder, 1934, prison, Deer Lodge, Montana. *Montana Historical Society.*

Bressien, who would later report that the same car had come back for more gas with only the man inside. Then the car and the man and apparently Adams had all disappeared.[85]

The attendant had been unable to supply an adequate description of the man in the car, leaving authorities little more to go on than Laura Adams's car, of which they had detailed information. The car was soon discovered in a garage in Butte, where Silver Bow authorities were able to shed light on the identity of the unknown man. It was believed that an arrest of the man would be made within thirty-six hours. At the finding of the car, Adams was still missing, but on August 19, the body of a woman was discovered twelve miles south of Logan. First being described as "in bad shape," Adams's face was later reported to have been beaten more than once with a hammer. Her body had been hidden under brush. Adams's son, Charles, shared that his mother usually carried a considerable sum on her person; however, no money had been found on the body or in the purse that had been left in the car.[86]

While the search for Adams's slayer continued, the coroner's jury ruled her cause of death as a blow to the head with a blunt instrument by an unknown person. Dr. R.R. Sigler testified that any one of the three blows would have been fatal. The mystery man was now known as Ed Stallings, a name that had been given at the Crowley Ranch south of Three Forks, where a man matching the murderer's description had been employed.

This name aligned with the testimony of a person who remembered Adams calling the man she left with "Eddie."[87]

On August 22, Calvert (Eddie) Stallings was arrested between Butte and Dillon by two sheriffs of Silver Bow County. The man had been pitching hay on a farm when apprehended, apparently trying to blend back into the farmhand life. A tip from an anonymous woman had led officers to that particular farm. At first, he had given his name to the officers as Charley Harris, but he had immediately admitted to the murder of Adams, claiming self-defense. According to Stallings, he had fallen asleep in the car and awoken to Adams going through his pockets. A struggle had ensued during which Adams had picked up a hammer. Stallings had gotten it away from her. "I hit her once," he said. "She raised up, so I thought I had better finish her off." Stallings would be held in a Butte jail for a day or so while Gallatin County attorney W.W. Lessley filed official charges of first-degree murder. Stallings was then transferred to the Gallatin County jail.[88]

A photograph of Stallings appeared in the *Independent Record* of Helena, Montana, where the man was shown sitting in an office surrounded by authorities and an attorney who was questioning him. According to the caption, he had been captured in only overalls and shoes while working, so

The car of Laura Adams, found in a Butte garage. *Gallatin Historical Society/Gallatin History Museum.*

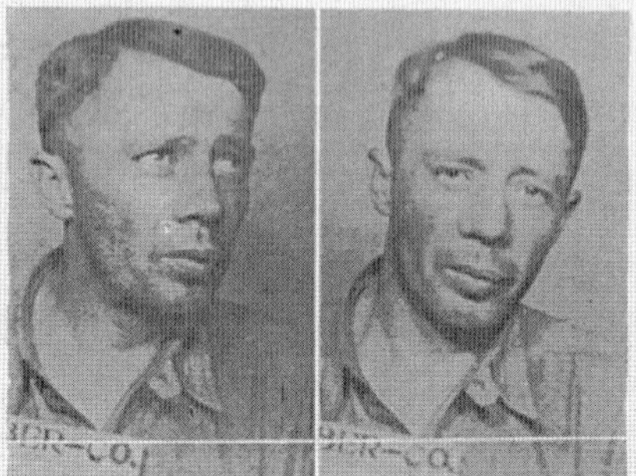

SHERIFF'S OFFICE, GALLATIN COUNTY, BOZEMAN, MONT.

WANTED ON CHARGE OF MURDER

Calvert Stallings, with aliases: Ted Stallings, Ed Stallings, Ed Harris, C. A. Harris.

F.P.C.	1	R	11	17	Ref.	1	R	111	17
	3	—	M	13		1	U	110	13

Description: Age about 35 to 45 years; 5 feet 6 or 7 inches: 150 to 160 lbs.; brown hair; slender build; has but one tooth on upper jaw and that is a molar, he may have a few stub teeth; the two upper front teeth were pulled August 9th, 1941. Has five lower teeth; has tattoo of naked woman on right forearm, inside. He is a farm laborer, and will probably be roughly dressed. This man is wanted for the murder of a woman near Three Forks, Montana, on August 14th, 1941.

CANCELLED

This photograph was taken in about 1935, and his cheeks may look more sunken. If apprehended hold and notify collect. Will extradite. Lovitt I. Westlake, Sheriff, Bozeman, Montana.

A wanted notice for the capture of Calvert Stallings, 1941. *Gallatin Historical Society/Gallatin History Museum.*

a shirt had been provided for him by deputies. It was noted that the "killer" was "slight in stature and mild-mannered" and that he had immediately asked for something to eat. He was given a sack of sandwiches, which he held in the photo. According to the accompanying article, Stallings believed he had not just fallen asleep; he was sure he had been doped. The story of what occurred in the struggle was more developed in this interview. Stallings stated that when he had awoken to Adams going through his pockets, he had pushed her away and hopped out of the car. She had come at him, and he slapped her several times. She had then grabbed the hammer from the car and hit him in the shoulder, after which, Stallings reported, "things went kind of goofy—I must have been drugged from the drinks. I grabbed the hammer away from her and hit her then I hit her again…and again.…I knew she was dead. So I dragged her off the road and left her in a clover field." He had then taken ten dollars from under her stocking, which he said she had taken from him, nothing more, and threw the hammer off into a field a distance from the murder scene. He had then traveled to Butte, where he had gotten a room at a hotel. Early Saturday morning, he had been arrested and booked on an intoxication charge in the Butte jail under the name of Dudley. He had been released Sunday morning and been rearrested Friday on the murder charge.[89]

A search for the murder weapon was finally fruitful. It was located about sixty yards from where the body of Adams had been found. While Stallings had confessed to the murder, Attorney Lessley announced the man was going to plead not guilty when arraigned. Within days, a connection was made between Stallings and a similar murder that had occurred on December 4, 1940, in Utah. Mrs. Anna G. Hallen had been found dead in the basement of her bungalow, having been struck over the head with a hatchet. Her home had been ransacked; the apparent motive was robbery. She had been seventy-three years of age. It was believed an ex-convict who had once lived with the woman posing as her stepbrother may have been the killer, but the slayer was never caught. Utah authorities had requested that Stallings be questioned about his whereabouts at the time of the Hallen murder due to the similarities in motive and method. According to an interview with Attorney Lessley, Stallings had been in the area but had been working for his father in a lumber company and as a painter. It seems a firm connection could not be made, as little else came about from the questioning, or perhaps more would have been followed up on had Stallings not been put on trial for the Adams murder. In any case, the Hallen murder seems to have remained a mystery.[90]

The trial began on October 13. Nearly all the first two days were taken up in securing a jury for the case. The selected group was composed of six men and six women. In his opening statement, Lessley told the jury the prosecution would show that the hammer slaying of Mrs. Laura Adams had been a "cruel, deliberate and malicious taking of human life." Howard Lewis, the court-appointed attorney for Stallings, reserved his opening statements for following the completion of state's evidence. The only time that Stallings showed emotion was during Sheriff Lovitt Westlake's testimony of the accused's confession of murder when taken from Butte to Bozeman. While testimony was being heard about the last blow of the death hammer after Adams had fallen to the ground, Stallings had raised his head to proclaim loudly, "I never said that." The gas station attendant was able to positively identify Stallings in the courtroom, which seems almost insignificant given Westlake's previous testimony on Stallings's confession.[91]

A brief of the trial showed how the prosecution attempted to reveal through examinations how alert Stallings had been throughout the evening of the murder. Stallings had been able to tell where the car was, that it had been running and that he had placed the hammer in a paper bag and then thrown both away. He could remember where he had thrown them. He had also been seen alert enough to pay for the gas on the way out with Adams in the car. According to the prosecution, "all of these facts point to a clear and accurate mind, working undimmed by any doping" and that the timing of the incident left no chance of recovery from the said doping

The body of Laura Adams lying in a field of clover next to the Madison River, 1941.
Gallatin Historical Society/Gallatin History Museum.

Calvert Stallings, first-degree murder, 1941, prison, Deer Lodge, Montana. *Montana Historical Society.*

that evening. It was noted that the murder was most likely premeditated, that Stallings had recently inquired about a car and that he had been heard saying he would "marry the old girl" for her car. It was believed that Stallings had come up with a ruse to get Laura Adams to go out of town with him that night.[92]

At the close of the prosecution's evidence, Stallings's defense called for an acquittal, which was immediately denied. Final statements and the presentation of instructions to the jury followed. The jury began its decision-making at 3:47 p.m., coming to a verdict that night. Its announcement, however, was deferred until the morning, as Judge Berg, who was presiding over the case, lived in Livingston and needed time to return. The jury pronounced Stallings guilty, recommending life imprisonment as the punishment.[93]

This sentence was indeed given to Stallings, who was thirty-eight at the time of his admittance to Deer Lodge State Prison. The back of his prison sheet details his other crimes, which included rape at the age of twenty-three, for which his five-year sentence was terminated after two months; disturbing the peace; suspected robbery; petit larceny; and drunkenness. Each time his name had been slightly different and included Delbert, Ted, Calvert Jack and Calvert John Stallings.[94]

Eight years following this conviction, in October 1949, Stallings was eligible for parole. His case was approved by the state board of pardons to reduce his sentence from life to fourteen years, which made him eligible for parole. It seems he had been a model prisoner and had a job waiting for him in Utah when released. The previous December, this same case had been rejected. Lessley, who was now a judge, firmly took a stand against Stallings's release, believing he had had a fair and just trial and needed to serve the sentence. It seems Stallings was indeed released, and it's possible he is a match for a Calvert Stallings who died in Utah in 1965 at the age of sixty-two of natural causes. And so ends the muddied tale of Mrs. Laura Adams.

Chapter 5

OF UNSOUND MIND

MURDER IN A BOUT OF INSANITY

Paul, my boy Paul—he's dead. I killed him.
—Fred Dambres, sent to Warm Springs, 1919

The insanity plea is often used as a last resort by defense lawyers to keep their client from paying the greatest cost for their crimes. Temporary insanity is a hard idea to grasp. Taking someone's life isn't a natural thing to do; one must lose a part of sanity to commit such a crime. However, in some instances, like some of the cases to follow, insanity truly does take over the murderer.

The years 1919 and 1920 were big ones for murders: Harry Walker was found dead (see chapter 3), and Florence and John Sprouse became the victims of foul play (see chapter 7). But those years were also peculiar in charges of murder by insanity. On November 5, 1919, Richard Ward killed Fred Rogers without warning, and just weeks later, on November 24, Fred Dambres killed his son. Both would be charged with insanity, but only one would go to prison.

The murder of Fred Rogers was simply solved, without question. Between 7:30 and 8:00 p.m., Richard Ward arrived at the home of Rogers and knocked on the door. When Rogers opened the door, he received a full blast from a shotgun and fell at the feet of Ward, crying out, "Papa! Papa! I'm shot!" He died before any help could reach him. Ward made an immediate confession when found at his home and was taken to the county jail without hesitation. The only immediate motive for the killing was a dispute over $3.40 that Ward claimed Rogers owed him.[95]

According to testimony at the coroner's inquest, Ward had been at the home of Oswald Smith playing cards when he got up and picked up his shotgun to leave, stating he was going to go get the money owed him by Rogers or "get him." Smith stated he tried to follow Ward but lost him; however, he soon knew of the murder because Ward came running back into the house telling him what he had just done. Smith had gone to the Rogerses' home then, where he found Rogers dead. A second witness, Robert Young, only heard the shot but had been a close acquaintance of Ward's. In fact, Ward and his wife had been scheduled to visit the Youngs' home for a game of whist that evening. Ward and Young had shared a drink of whiskey earlier in the evening, and Young had invited the Wards to the game. It seems Ward had given no indication of his plans. Young had heard the shot and ran out of the house thinking someone had shot at Mrs. Harrison's dog (where the Youngs resided). When he saw nothing, he returned to the house.[96]

There had been four other people at the Rogers home when the murder occurred: Rogers's wife, friend Sam Heard, Heard's wife and Rogers's father. Rogers and Sam Heard had been playing checkers, and their wives had been busy in the home when they had heard the knock on the door. It was noticed but questioned till the third knock, when Rogers had gotten up from the checker game to open the door. Chaos had ensued and a doctor was called for in hopes that Rogers was still alive, but there had been little hope. A piece of Rogers's heart had been torn away; there had been nothing anyone could have done to save him, and he had died shortly after the blast. According to Smith, Ward had asked for a piece of paper following their card game, prior to his leaving for the Rogerses' home. He had written two notes, one to a Mrs. Mary McDonald of Bozeman (his mother) and one to his wife; they both said nearly the same: "Am very sorry this had to happen, but I cannot help it. Goodbye to all of you and love. Dick." This clearly showed the murder had been a premeditated attack.[97]

Richard Ward was only eighteen years of age, having just been married to Willie Burden (age twenty-one) that April with the consent of his mother. It was rumored that the marriage had been fraught with difficulties and possibly violence, as Ward carried a slight wound on his head at the time of his arrest. Fred Rogers had been thirty-one years old and well liked in the community. Both were born and raised in Bozeman.[98]

The trial progressed slowly in January 1920. All the aforementioned witnesses would be called to testify, Robert Young being called from the state penitentiary, where he was then serving a sentence for carrying concealed weapons (convicted November 14, 1919, in Miles City). Early on, it became clear that the defense was paving the way for a plea of insanity. Testimony was given by teachers at the Emerson School as to Ward's character, and mental measurements were even submitted by the principal of the school. Objections were made to this submission, but it is unknown if they were sustained. Local attorney Justin Smith and prominent citizen Nelson Story Jr. both testified to having known Ward, and both believed the man to be perfectly sane. Ward's grandmother then testified to him having frequent headaches and spells where he would seem "out of his head." Many other family members and a doctor were called to testify on this point. According to Dr. Blair, he believed at the time of the shooting, given Ward's history, he had been insane. A few other doctors put on the stand for the defense believed the same and that due to this mental disease of some sort he had been acting under irresistible impulse brought on by an overpowering of his mental state. When Ward had been asked by his mother why he had murdered Rogers, he had stated, "I had to do it."[99]

On January 14, the state rested its case, and the defense made its statement asserting that Ward had not been in his right mind when the murder occurred. In a surprise testimony by Sheriff Charles Esgar, it was disclosed that a noose had been found attached to Ward's sweater in his cell. An extra guard had been put on a suicide watch for young Ward. Following a trial that lasted eleven days, eleven of the twelve jurors voted

Emerson School. *Gallatin Historical Society/Gallatin History Museum.*

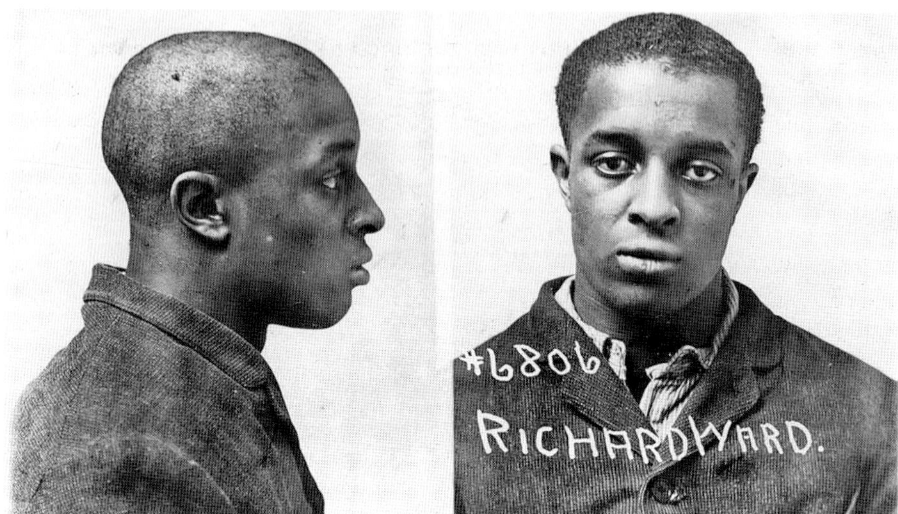

Richard Ward, second-degree murder, 1910, prison, Deer Lodge, Montana. *Montana Historical Society*.

for first-degree murder and nine of those for the death penalty. Only one man voted for second-degree murder, holding out long enough that the jury decided to give in to his vote rather than let a disagreement ensue. Ward seemed a lucky man in light of such a grave and premeditated offense.[100]

Judge B.B. Law, however, was not impressed by the defense's evidence of insanity, saying as much in his sentencing of the young Ward. Law called notice to the defense's attempts to show that Ward had been behind at school, stating it was not clear if this was a sign of mental deficiency or a lack of application on the part of Ward. Law also called attention to the two notes Ward had written prior to the murder, the bringing of a shotgun with him to Smith's house, the threats made to Rogers previously and the success of losing Smith on his trail to the Rogerses' home as clear signs of premeditation, not irresistible impulse. According to Law, he could not believe that Ward did not know right from wrong but that Ward needed to undergo considerable change to keep him from being a threat to society. But Law did see hope, so he chose a sentence with the potential for leniency of parole should Ward prove himself a "useful citizen."[101]

The *Billings Weekly Gazette* reported the sentence Judge Law pronounced on Ward in an article titled "$3.40 Murderer Gets Long Term" on January 29.[102] Ward was found guilty of second-degree murder and sentenced to not less than thirty-seven and a half years and not more than seventy-five years in the prison. At the time, this was the longest sentence ever given in this part of Montana. At the earliest, he would have been released in 1957 at the age of fifty-six; however, it seems he may have been released much earlier. On November 9, 1937, Richard Ward died in Bozeman of pulmonary and spinal tuberculosis, of which he had been suffering for over a year. He was buried in the Sunset Hills Cemetery. According to the death certificate, it states he was widowed. Willie Ward had died following an operation at the age of twenty-six, just a few years after Ward was sent to prison in 1924. It is unknown what became of Rogers's wife.[103]

The case of Fred Dambres, who killed his own son just weeks following the Ward murder, went quite differently. Fred had been committed to the Warm Springs Sanitarium two years previously but had recently been released and considered completely cured. Fred had been living in a cabin separate from his sons at the time of the shooting, apparently living under the paranoid suspicion that his sons were trying to poison him. It seems some part of his insanity remained as some level of paranoia.

On the night of the murder at about six o'clock, Fred had been at his cabin in Bridger Canyon when his son Paul knocked on the door. Paul had recently gotten off work and had come home to dinner, which his brother Adolph had ready. He was told that their father had taken the sugar, so Paul had gone to visit Fred in hopes of retaining some. Paul knocked on the door and then kicked it before his father appeared at the small glass window in the door, through which he shot Paul with a shotgun. Adolph, who was a few steps away, witnessed the whole thing, including his brother turning toward him after the shot and walking a few steps before falling to the ground and almost immediately dying. Adolph had taken his brother back to their cabin before setting out for the Rabe Ranch three miles away for help. The sheriff was notified, but due to bad roads, it was after midnight before a posse and the coroner arrived at the ranch. From there, they were taken by sleigh out to the Dambres cabins.[104]

The posse was able to capture Fred without much of a struggle; the man had been found pacing back and forth in his cabin. When asked where Paul was, he said, "Paul, my boy Paul—he's dead. I killed him." He then related how it had been his duty to kill Paul because the boy had been hiding things from him. It was soon related by Adolph that Fred had been in a rage for a week or so, in some part due to Paul hiding the coffee from his father as he had been drinking large quantities of black coffee, which the boys thought might be harmful to him. Fred had instead believed that his boys were trying to poison him and as such had stopped eating with them at their cabin. Fred

Maiden Rock at the mouth of Bridger Canyon, 1924. *Gallatin Historical Society/Gallatin History Museum.*

would claim that Paul had been trying to break into his cabin to kill him when he had fired his shot in self-defense. He blamed the broken glass on Paul; however, powder burns on the back of the door indicated that the shot, not Paul, had busted the glass and door.[105]

The entire party headed to Bozeman, bringing Paul's body back on a sled. Paul had been twenty-four years of age, the second oldest of five children. Adolph was the third oldest. Charles (the eldest), Peter and Emma had all been living with their mother in Bozeman so they could attend school. The family was from Poland, and Paul had recently spent time at Camp Lewis prior to the armistice being signed. He had since worked on a road gang building bridges in the Bridger Canyon. It was said that he was "quiet, steady and an extremely good farm hand."[106]

The next mention of the sad affair was on January 28, when it was announced that Fred Dambres would be undergoing a sanity hearing prior to a charge of murder. This was a very different approach from that of the Richard Ward case, where a plea of insanity was only introduced during the murder trial itself by the defense. It may be because Fred was already confirmed mentally unstable by his two-year stint at Warm Springs. If Fred was determined sane at the hearing, he would remain confined in the county jail until his trial for murder; if not, then he would be returned to Warm Springs. The catch was if he regained his sanity again at the asylum, he would have to return to Bozeman to face trial for the murder of his son. Justice could not be escaped for Paul's death. In the end, Fred was found to be insane during the time of the shooting and was sent back to Warm Springs. Interestingly, his wife's death certificate, dated 1935, indicates that she died at the Montana State Hospital at Warm Springs. It is possible she stayed with him at the hospital on occasion or became ill while visiting, as her address was still listed as Bozeman. But it seems that Fred Dambres never again left the institution. His death certificate could not be located. One notes on Paul's death certificate, filled out four days following the shooting, that Paul's cause of death was "gunshot wound fired by insane father." It seems there was little doubt as to what had truly occurred.[107]

On June 3, 1938, Montanans woke up to a startling headline. "Jury Charges Kunze Killed Mayor, Wife." The shooting had taken place the night before, at the home of August and Louise Kunze, the Three Forks mayor and his wife. The killer, John Kunze, was the half brother of the mayor. Already a coroner's jury had charged John Kunze with the murder; the inquest had been held the day following the deaths. Testimony at the inquest included that of Howard Nelson, county coroner, and witnesses

17 I HEREBY CERTIFY, That I attended deceased from ...., 19........, to.., 19........,

that I last saw h............alive on.., 19........,

and that death occurred, on the date stated above, at....................m.

The CAUSE OF DEATH* was as follows:

died from gunshot wound

fired by insane father

The death certificate of Paul Dambres, November 24, 1919. *Ancestry.com.*

including Edward Groves of Three Forks, who had been talking with the Kunzes when the shots were fired. According to Groves, he saw a man come up the street with a rifle. When he got within fifty feet, he had thrown the rifle to his shoulder; said, "Hands up"; and fired. The first shot took Mrs. Kunze and the second, the mayor, who had cried out, "Don't shoot!" and started to turn away. The rifle was a .30-06 and fully loaded and cocked when John Kunze was apprehended along with ten clips of cartridges in an ammunition belt.[108]

Held in the county jail, Kunze did not hold back on his admission of guilt. In fact, he felt no remorse and was quoted as saying, "I feel that I have done my duty. It is what a man should do in life." Reports from the *Billings Gazette* told more of the story. Following the shooting, John Kunze had barricaded himself in his home with his aged mother. He was driven out with tear gas bombs fired by Bozeman and Butte officials. Kunze's mother had escaped the home when the first bomb was fired, but Kunze had fired two wild shots and then had gone to the basement. He was soon caught attempting to leave through a window on the first floor. He was handcuffed by Sheriff Lovitt Westlake and a Butte sheriff while he was still halfway through the window.[109]

According to an interview in the Billings paper, Kunze had originally planned to kill the couple on May 29 but had taken the opportunity to do it earlier when he saw them together through the window of his home. He had used field glasses to ensure it was them and then went straight over. He stated, "I wanted to get them both at once. Not one at a time."[110] It seems that the mayor had once brought Kunze in for a sanity hearing in 1931, but he had been declared sane. In all comments on the shooting, his reasoning just seemed to be he wanted "out of the well" that they had put him in.

Clerk of District Court records room and vault at the old Gallatin County Courthouse, pre-1938. *Gallatin Historical Society/Gallatin History Museum.*

The trial of Kunze would be delayed due to his difficulty obtaining counsel. He was given additional time to enter his plea. Seth Bohart would eventually become Kunze's defense attorney and intended to base the defense on insanity on behalf of his client. The case opened on October 10, with the star witness, Groves, on the stand. He told the story of how the murders had occurred, adding that following the shooting, Kunze had turned to him and said, "The rest of you go about your business, I got the two I want." Interestingly, in his opening statements, county attorney Landoe told the jury he expected a verdict of guilty of murder in the first degree, but it did not seem like he would ask for the death penalty.[111]

The testimony of Dr. H.W. Gregg, a psychiatrist from Butte, intended to prove Kunze's insanity. According to Dr. Gregg, he had had examined Kunze in 1927 in Butte and had then advised the family to seek institutional help for the man. Just prior to this testimony Kunze himself had taken the stand to explain why he had murdered the couple. His statements were rambling and bizarre. He stated: "I was working under a system which had several branches and each one of these branches had a certain meaning or rule that should be followed if anything was disturbed…when I got my rules and regulations why, I took them up right there and I see that the time said that I should go and shoot these two parties to even up the time." He went on to state that he had not been angry or upset with his half brother and his wife and that they weren't to blame. He said that they did not know they had broken the "rule."[112]

While the jury brought back a verdict of guilty, Kunze was made to wait weeks to hear his sentencing as physicians conferred on his current mental state. Finally on October 24, Kunze was sentenced to life in prison. He was asked by Judge Berg, "Do you believe, that after taking the lives of two innocent people that you, yourself, should be allowed to live?" to which Kunze had replied, "Yes, I really do judge."[113]

Kunze spent twenty-three years in prison, dying there at the age of sixty-two in 1961. The mayor and his wife at the time of their deaths left behind two daughters, aged eleven and eight years old. Interestingly, Louise's death certificate says "married," while August's says "widowed," as Louise had died just seconds before him.

Chapter 6

I SHOT THE SHERIFF

RUNNING FROM THE LAW

We got him.
—Sheriff Esgar on the death of Buford Webb, 1919

It's the quintessential western setup: the bad guys go on the run, a posse is brought together and one knows that those they chase don't have a chance of coming in alive, particularly if they've killed someone like the deputy sheriff.

In January 1897, Gallatin County was experiencing a dose of excitement. Unfortunately, it was of a dark kind. Frank Morgan, alias John Streator, had beaten a P.T. Colthar of Salesville, stolen horses and managed to escape the grip of Sheriff W.J. Fransham. Following his escape, he had been joined by Harvey Whitton, another troublesome character. The two were discovered in Al Carpenter's cabin at Cherry Creek by Fransham and Deputy Jack Allen. It seems the small posse of two had left their horses in the stable before going to the cabin, from which Carpenter emerged. They questioned the man about the two desperados, to which Carpenter stated that they were inside and would not be taken alive. At this, one of the men appeared at the door, stating the same. When Allen approached after having tied up the horses, the man at the door suddenly and without warning fired a shot at Allen, taking him down in his tracks. Another shot was then fired at Fransham, but he managed to escape with only minor injuries. Fransham had made a run for the brush but was overpowered and stripped of his gun and money by the desperados. He was allowed to carry Allen inside the cabin, where the men told him to stay until after dark. Somehow a messenger was sent for a doctor, and Fransham was soon organizing a posse back at Salesville. When Fransham left Allen, he was still able to talk, but it was believed his wounds were considerable. Upon examination by Dr. Chambliss, it was found the situation for Allen was dire. Buckshot had struck through his temple to the back of his eye, fracturing his skull, and some of the metal could not be located.[114]

Sheriff W.F. Fransham, 1897–1901. *Gallatin Historical Society/ Gallatin History Museum.*

Posses quickly assembled in Ennis, Virginia City and Manhattan amounting to fifty men. According to the *Anaconda Standard*, these men were "armed with Winchester rifles and filled with determination to bring back the carcasses of the two desperadoes."[115] However, after five days the men were still on the search, with some of the parties having given up. The Salesville posse remained on the scene, scouring the area around Cottonwood Canyon where Deputy Allen's cartridges were found, having been taken by the desperadoes following his shooting. Sheriff Fransham, however, made his search around Virginia City, where he had gotten a few clues, the meaning of which was not stated in the paper. Deputy Allen had finally arrived in Bozeman, and it was believed that the doctor had hopes for his recovery.[116]

The shooting of Deputy Allen had occurred on January 14; thirteen days later, the search had turned up empty, and it was believed they had escaped the area. Fransham released a detailed description of the two men to be circulated widely across Montana. Frank Morgan, alias John Streator, was described as "five feet, six inches, weighing about 136 pounds, smooth shaved, dark blue or grey eyes, long thin, aquiline nose, sharp, thin features, slightly stoop shouldered and 23 years of age. He has small feet and hands, about number six shoe or boot (cowboy style) legs slightly bowed and toes slightly turned out when walking, brown hair, wears sometimes a black felt hat, sometimes a white cowboy hat." It was also noted he had a peculiarity of his usually flushed face turning white when he smiled, "as though frost bitten" and that he had several disguises. Harvey Whitton was dark complexioned and believed to be a quarter or eighth African American. According to Fransham's description, he was

"20 years old, five feet, 10 inches high and weighs 160 pounds." It was also noted he had light hair, dark eyes, a flat nose, thick lips, heavy jaws, a frowning expression and slightly bowed legs and wore size eight boots. A $400 reward, $200 from Fransham and $200 from Sheriff Joseph Haines of Madison County, had been offered for their capture.[117]

While it seems Fransham and Haines were in unison on this case, further reading of an article in the *Anaconda Standard* shows a different side. Haines had been alerted almost immediately by telegram of the escaping duo and again of the shooting of Jack Allen, yet when Fransham first arrived in Virginia City, he found Haines had done nothing to apprehend the men. In fact, Haines had not even mentioned the situation to anyone, a serious disregard of his post, as the shooting of Allen had actually occurred in Madison County, his jurisdiction not Fransham's. It is due to Fransham's diligence in protesting Haines's negligence that Haines saw his error and offered a $200 reward. But the help was too late on Haines's part, for the desperadoes had been given a golden opportunity to escape. It was believed that the charge of first-degree assault on the men would be changed to first-degree murder in time. Deputy Allen was still in critical condition, and hope for his recovery was starting to dwindle.[118]

On February 2, nineteen days after being shot, Jack Allen succumbed to his wounds. It was said that Allen suffered great pain and convulsions during that time; there had been little that could be done for him other than to try to make him as comfortable as possible. It seems Allen was able to speak during those long days and often repeated to his friends and fellow officers: "My gun snapped. If my gun hadn't snapped it would have been different." The bullet, which had not been found when Allen was alive, was discovered in a postmortem. It had passed through his brain, creating a laceration that became inflamed, causing his death. An avengement of his death was wished by all in the town. Allen had been thirty-seven years of age.[119]

In October 1897, Whitton was picked up in Nevada and taken to Virginia City for trial. While awaiting trial, Whitton very nearly made his escape from the Virginia City jail, but his scheme, planned with two other prisoners, was discovered by a sheriff stepping on a loose floorboard. His trial would take place in March 1898, over a year following the murder of Jack Allen. At the trial, it was noted that following the shooting, Whitton had wanted to kill Fransham on the spot, but Morgan had stopped him. Allen's own premortem admission that Whitton had shot him was struck from the evidence, as Allen had suffered brain injuries and his judgment had been skewed. On the stand, Whitton of course pleaded that Morgan had fired the

Deputy Jack Allen. *Gallatin Historical Society/Gallatin History Museum.*

shot that killed Allen. A principal witness for the prosecution, a George Brooks of Nevada, whom Whitton confessed the murder to, was somehow kept from the trial. Morgan was never caught or tried for Allen's murder, but Whitton was charged with second-degree murder and sentenced to eighty years at Deer Lodge.[120]

In 1910, Whitton received parole, a case won by his sister, Miss Dolly Whitton, an inmate of the Young Women's Christian Home for the Blind. It seems she had only recently learned of her brother's plight from her mother, who let known her son's secret on her deathbed. To gain his parole, Whitton wrote a statement from prison in which he detailed the situation that had occurred in 1897. According to his statement, he had been wanted for hitting a man over the head with the butt of a revolver during an argument. He had met up with Morgan and told him his troubles, letting Morgan know the officers were after him and not to make trouble. Whitton states that Morgan shot Allen and then held up and robbed Fransham while Whitton was dragged along as an accomplice. Whitton had applied for pardon, but the case had been refused. Parole was the only option left to him, as he had served a portion of his sentence. This he was granted. He never did go to live with his sister, though, as was the plan upon his release. Instead, his life of crime continued. Within two years of his parole, Whitton was back in prison, this time at the Nevada Penitentiary sentenced to one to fourteen years for horse stealing. It seems his time in prison was also not idle; it is believed that he masterminded murder and a dynamiting ransom scheme against the Northern Pacific Railroad all from his prison cell. It is unknown what became of Frank Morgan.[121]

In late January 1915, Three Forks city marshal John Dolan was killed by a bullet through his heart. The killer was Frank Durham, a well-known rancher and, as noted by the *Missoulian*, the son of wealthy people. According to reports, the whole affair had been a mistake. It seems Marshal Dolan had mistaken Durham for someone named "Jim" whom he intended to arrest. When Durham resisted, the marshal had started beating him over the head with his club. Durham had fired his gun in self-defense, thinking the officer was going to kill him. As though to corroborate the story, the *Missoulian* also noted that at the time of writing, Durham was confined to a bed due to the beating he had undergone.[122] By mid-February, Durham had returned to his ranch north of Belgrade, out on $35,000 bail for first-degree murder.[123] It was believed by all that when it came time for trial, his plea would be self-defense.

The trial began in late March, with nearly a whole day given to the testimony of Bess Miller, proprietor of the house of ill repute where the shooting had occurred. This detail had been missing from earlier reports of the incident. According to Bess Miller, Frank Durham and Pearl Wells had been at Miller's home from Monday evening until Wednesday morning, the day of the shooting. Apparently Marshal Dolan had the custom of checking in on Bess Miller's house every evening. That particular visit (at 2:30 a.m.) was fraught with conflict. Dolan had been in a rage against an Amy Howard of Logan, whom he had found there. He had sworn at both her and Bess Miller before entering the bedroom where Durham and Pearl Wells were seated. He immediately attempted to force Durham to go with him; however, Durham resisted, and the beating had ensued. By this time, Durham had been forced into the kitchen by Dolan, where they were alone in their struggle. Bess Miller testified to hearing a shot fired and then shortly after a second shot. When she arrived on the scene, Dolan was breathing his last. Both Durham and Pearl Wells had left the house soon after the shooting had occurred, but Bess Miller had not known where they had gone.[124]

The four "girls" that had been in the house at the time of the shooting—Gail Ward, Ruth Adams, Amy Howard and Pearl Wells—were not called to the stand by the state. The defense attorney for Durham requested they be called, but the state declined; the issue was resolved when it was decided the defense could call them instead. The testimony of these women was not shared in the papers, as it was noted that what they said was similar to the testimony of Bess Miller. Later that same year, Pearl Wells and Amy Howard would be arrested with eight other women for being inmates of a prostitution house. Most, including Pearl Wells, would pay a one-hundred-dollar fine.[125]

Another day was centered on the characters of both Durham and Dolan. Ed Reynolds, former sheriff of Gallatin County, was called to testify on having known Dolan for many years. Reynolds stated that Dolan was "quick tempered, brutal and a dangerous man; that he unnecessarily used his billy club and his gun." The same was reiterated by James O'Keefe, who had known Dolan in Anaconda, along with three other witnesses. A few more were called who testified the opposite, saying they had heard nothing of

Dolan's brutality. A slate of witnesses was then questioned as to the character of Durham, all reporting that he was good and that he was a quiet, law-abiding citizen.[126]

Sheriff Ed M. Reynolds, 1906–9. *Gallatin Historical Society/Gallatin History Museum.*

On April 3, the jury returned a verdict of not guilty. The jury had included Alfred Schlechten, a well-known Bozeman photographer. The trial had been presided over by Judge B.B. Law. Durham would quickly grace headlines again just days after his acquittal when he was arrested in Logan at "the resort" of Pearl Wells. Charges were not filed, and Durham was released on his own recognizance, although the arrest nevertheless caused quite a stir. The *Butte Inner-Mountain* reported that Durham would be given thirty days on a vagrancy charge. The charge is an odd one, and it is unknown if he served the time or paid some fine.[127]

Twenty-two years following the death of Deputy Jack Allen, two deputies were killed by "deranged farm hand" Buford Webb in a six-hour gunfight. It seems the trouble had started ten days before the battle, when Webb had made his intentions known to his employer, Harvey Plumlee, that he was going to quit. When he asked for his wages, he disagreed with the amount owed him by Plumlee and threatened to kill his employer, once with a gun and once with a knife. Both times Plumlee had escaped harm. Webb was apprehended and taken to the county jail to await charges of threatening a person and carrying concealed weapons. His trial in Manhattan found him guilty, and he was charged fifty dollars for the weapon offense. He was then released.[128]

On October 11, 1919, shortly after the noon hour, Plumlee approached a granary building on his property to use his pumping station. Webb had suddenly burst out from the building, leveled his rifle at Plumlee and fired. Plumlee had been able to turn to start fleeing because the first shot had gone wild, but the second hit him in the back of his left shoulder. He had fallen but regained his footing and ran to a nearby ranch for help. Five more shots were fired, but none took effect. Plumlee was able to contact Manhattan deputy sheriff Frank Curtice, who in turn telephoned Sheriff Charles Esgar in Bozeman, who told Curtice to "go, get him." Curtice had then summoned local help, deputizing the men who formed his posse.

These men included Pomeroy Vreeland, a good friend of Curtice's whom Curtice just happened to run into on the street that day; Frank Collins; and Frank Jakle. The four men drove to the Plumlee ranch, stopping one hundred yards away. Collins and Jakle stayed behind at the car while Curtice and Vreeland advanced. Almost immediately, Webb shot through the window of an old cabin, hitting both men. Both fell, mortally wounded. At the time, it was unclear if both men were dead; it was said Vreeland moved once or twice, and it was hoped that they had been "shamming" to escape Webb. It was later discovered that Curtice had taken a bullet to his forehead, dying instantly, and that Vreeland had turned to run and taken a bullet to his back that had passed through above his heart, most likely killing him almost instantly. Neither Collins nor Jakle were able to approach them without being fired on by Webb.[129]

Jakle was sent for help while Collins remained on guard to ensure Webb did not escape. Within a half hour it was reported that one hundred men had arrived on the scene, surrounding the granary where Webb had now barricaded himself. It would be another half hour before Sheriff Esgar and deputies would arrive from Bozeman. Esgar gave Webb the chance to surrender and was answered by shots, leaving the posse little choice in the matter. The situation would take six hours in full to come to an end. During that time, several pigs had to be killed by the posse to protect the bodies of Vreeland and Curtice from mutilation. The granary was riddled with bullets for hours, much of the attack coming from a giant haystack near the granary. Silence from the granary told the men that Webb may be dead. It seems a young lad snuck up to a window to look in, waving to the others to come. It was said that they found Webb still alive with multiple bullet wounds but that he died within minutes.[130]

However, other stories would be circulated regarding the death of Webb. According to the *Bozeman Courier*, other attempts were made to enter the granary during the standoff. Someone had suggested burning Webb out of the building, so telephone wire was cleverly strung from hill to hill over the building to which gunnysacks soaked with oil were attached. These were set on fire, creating a barrage of smoke. Using this smoke as a cover, some of the posse was able to approach close enough to the granary to place dynamite in a position to blow up a corner of the building. It was said a noise was heard inside the building following the explosion, and it was later evident that Webb may have been perched up on a rafter inside the building when the explosion took place. The rafters had been blood soaked, showing he had been injured at the time, and his body was later found to be badly

Left: Sheriff Chas. C. Esgar, 1919–23. *Gallatin Historical Society/Gallatin History Museum.*

Below: The Plumlee ranch, showing where the bodies of Vreeland and Curtice were found (1 and 2) and the granary where Webb was killed (3). *Gallatin Historical Society/Gallatin History Museum.*

bruised, probably from the fall. What followed differed greatly in stories reported in papers around Montana. According to the *Courier*, some say the sound of gunfire followed as members of the posse entered the building and "when the balance of the posse came up Webb was found with a bullet through his forehead." Some say Webb was on his knees with his rifle when they entered; some say he was on his side ready to shoot. Some believe that he was surrendering. But evidence clearly shows that, whatever his position, he was given no chance to survive. Upon examination, Webb had nine wounds, two of which would have proved fatal.[131]

In the days following the tragedy, new light would be shed on the murderer Buford Webb and what had occurred in the granary that day. If anything, it only made the story more confusing. According to an article in the *Bozeman Courier*, Webb had been in the granary, not the barn, when he had fired at Curtis and Vreeland. It seems neither Curtice nor Vreeland had been armed in this account. When the two had fallen victim to Webb, the remaining two—sometimes called McGaffey and Collins, sometimes Jakle and Collins—had fired into the granary, and it had been then that they had heard a body fall, indicating that Webb may have been at that moment incapacitated enough that if the building had been rushed, he could have been taken in quickly. However, according to the paper, the two remaining would have had no way of knowing this and thus help was obtained instead. This accounting differs greatly from those previously told.[132]

The reasons behind Webb's attack also were speculated on. According to the *Courier*, following his arrest, he had talked to Coroner Gray, in his capacity as attorney, where Gray concluded that Webb was a sick man. According to Gray, as Webb left, he had said, "Someone ought to take a gun and get that ——." Gray was careful in his interview with the *Courier* to state that he had no real inkling that Webb was going to follow through on his threats. Gray believed the man to be insane at the time of the shooting of Plumlee. According to Gray, only an insane man would have stayed in the area following the shooting when he had ample time to escape. Following Webb's death, Gray, in his capacity as coroner, found two checks in the pockets of Webb, both made out for $210 to himself, both unsigned. One was from the Manhattan State Bank and the other from the Home State Bank. It was thought that Webb had intended to force Plumlee to sign the checks, hence why the first shot had missed the man. When Plumlee ran, Webb tried to stop him with a bullet.[133]

It was also believed that Webb had Industrial Workers of the World connections taken on during his wanderings. According to the *Courier*, a

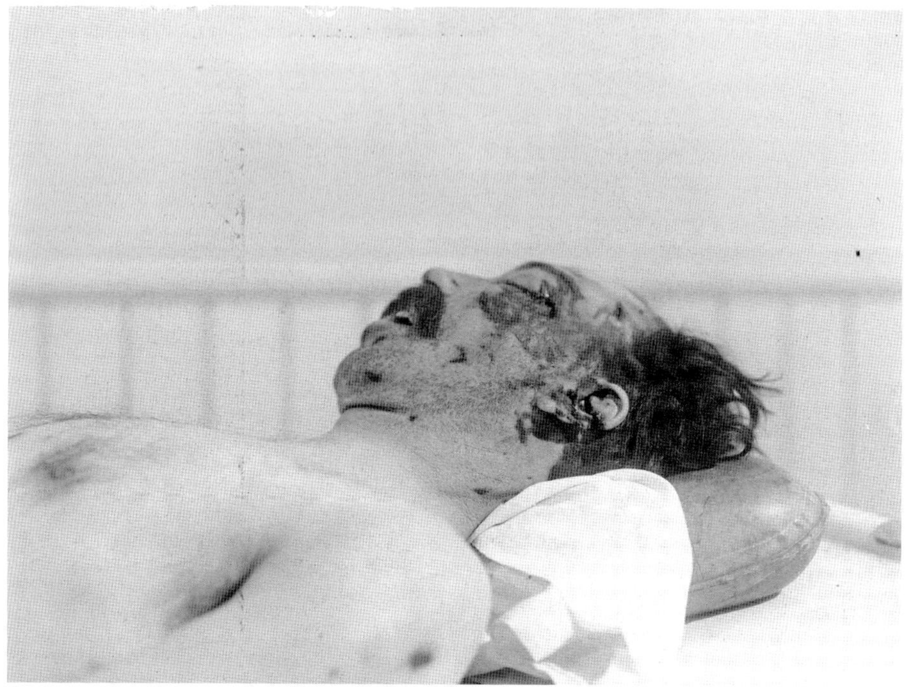

Buford Webb at the undertaker. *Gallatin Historical Society/Gallatin History Museum.*

diary was found in Webb's pocket that alluded to his rambling lifestyle. It was noted that he had written in the diary, following the shooting of Plumlee, that he had "gloried in the deed and looked upon the approaching battle as something to be enjoyed." Whether this is true may never be known, as it is unknown what became of the diary. It was said that he had ample ammunition and provisions in the building to last quite a while. Why he had chosen a run-down building was never explained.[134]

In any event, the body of Buford Webb, age twenty-six, was sent back to his hometown of Ludlow, Missouri. Deputy Frank Curtice, age thirty-nine, was buried in Manhattan. Curtice left behind a wife and large hole in the community. He had been deputy sheriff at Manhattan and Logan, Manhattan town marshal and city clerk and a member of the Independent Order of Odd Fellows. Pomeroy Vreeland had been a Bozeman native whose father had been an architect in the area. Upon the death of his father, Byron, the family had made their way back east, where Pomeroy had taken up the architect trade, studying in Michigan and Chicago. He had returned to Bozeman, where he had worked with local renowned architect Fred Willson. Pomeroy left behind a wife as well.[135]

Above: The granary where Buford Webb met his end. *Gallatin Historical Society/Gallatin History Museum.*

Right: Pomeroy Vreeland. *Gallatin Historical Society/Gallatin History Museum.*

The watch carried by Buford Webb that was broken by a bullet, authenticated by the official letter from the sheriff's office, and a piece of the granary building with a bullet hole. *Image by Victoria Richard; Gallatin Historical Society/Gallatin History Museum.*

In a reminiscence by Francis Niven, who was a young child at the time of the Webb incident, Francis recalls having seen Webb on occasion, once cursing profusely at some horses while treating them roughly. According to Francis, on the day of the shooting, there had been a knock on the door of the Heeb School. The Plumlee children were called out, but nothing was said to the rest. Soon after, the children could hear "round after round of heavy rifle fire" coming from the west, which continued sporadically throughout the day. Late that evening, when a procession of cars had started to come by, Francis and his father had gone down to the edge of the road to see what the outcome had been. According to Francis, the sheriff was in the lead, and "as he drove by, he slowed down, turned in his seat, and motioned with his left hand into the back seat of the car, and shouted 'we got him.'" They had simply wrapped Webb in a blanket and dumped him in the back of the car.[136]

Chapter 7

MAY GOD HAVE MERCY ON YOUR SOUL

EXECUTIONS

I leave my story for the courts to furnish the final.
—John A. Clark, executed for first-degree murder, 1884

Prior to 1884, three hangings had been conducted in Gallatin County, none of them legally. In 1864, Bill Hunter, a road agent, was hanged by vigilantes from Virginia City. On the night of January 31, 1873, "Steamboat Bill" and Z.T. Tripplett were pulled from the Bozeman jail and lynched on a meat rack just outside town. As more people came to the valley and the law enforcement team grew, the punishment for crime was doled out in a more civilized manner. One would be given a trial prior to such conduct. Whether those trials were fair is up for consideration.

The first legal execution in Gallatin County occurred on January 1, 1884. John A. Clark was hanged for the murder of T. Rogers—the motive, robbery. It seems in the summer of 1883 Clark had purposefully made the acquaintance of T. Rogers and Peter Lyman, who were former railroad workers heading for the Clarks Fork Mines near Cooke City. Their last job in Bozeman had netted them about $800, which Rogers carried on his person. It was at a chance encounter in an establishment at Rocky Canyon that Clark first caught a glimpse of Rogers's bankroll while the latter was purchasing liquor. This sight prompted him to strike up a conversation with the men and, finding their sense of geography of the region to which they were headed lacking, offered himself up as a guide. Clark proceeded them to a place called Mountain House where he pawned his gun before the

Vigilante hanging of Z.T. Triplett and John St. Clair ("Steamboat Bill") on January 31, 1873. *Gallatin Historical Society/Gallatin History Museum.*

grouping headed out. When they reached Pine Creek, just five miles from the Yellowstone Valley, they stopped, Clark stating that this was the best camping spot. He then asked Rogers to accompany him out fishing, telling him to bring a gun, as they might see black-tailed deer in that area. Lyman stayed behind but soon heard three shots ring out. He headed up the creek, along the way meeting Clark, who asked for a hatchet or axe with which to butcher the deer he said they had killed. Lyman was for some reason immediately suspicious. He went back to camp; left a note on a scrap of paper reading, "T. Rogers: Stay in camp till I get back"; and then he went up Trail Creek to a cabin owned by Congers Smith where he spent the night.[137]

The following day, he found the camp undisturbed, but the horses were gone. He then got Smith, and the two searched up Pine Creek for Rogers. It did not take long for them to find Rogers's body with two bullet wounds to the head, one near the chin and one under the jaw. Oddly, his suspenders had been removed and tied about his neck, a setup it seems Clark had used to drag the body about sixty steps. Rogers had been relieved of most of his money; however, one roll of $250 had been left untouched in a pocket.[138]

Help was soon secured by means of Justice Davis, who put out a warrant for Clark's arrest. The case was given to Constable Hineman. Within about a day, Clark was caught. A tip from Mr. White Calfee about Clark's interest in a Miss Hawks who lived near Livingston proved fruitful. It was there that Clark was caught with money he had not had at Mountain House, where he had been destitute. Clark came quietly; however, he professed his innocence to the gallows. According to Clark, he had journeyed with the group and had camped that night at Pine Creek. He declared he had wanted to go to town that night, but the grouping had said he should stay with them. Along the way, Clark stated he purchased a horse from a man named Thompson, whom they saw multiple times along the trail. On the morning when Rogers's body was found, Clark said that he had gone into Livingston and from there to Hawks's place, where he was arrested, which was his first time hearing the news of Rogers's death. In a letter to the *Chronicle*, he stated: "I leave my story for the courts to furnish the final."[139]

The *Chronicle* published a long article on Clark's life, furnished himself in a letter, which detailed his movements from March 1868, when he first left Virginia for California, through the day of the murder. The meeting of Rogers and Lyman was outlined, including how Clark had helped the men pack for their journey to the mines. There were few details of the trial published, but according to Clark, following his conviction and just a day prior to his execution, he had nothing but kind words for the sheriffs and guards, especially Sheriff Blakley. He believed the district attorney had done "nothing but his duty" and said, "Peace be with the judge and jury."[140]

His letters to the *Chronicle* and three to relatives were written the night before his execution. In one he wrote: "To-night I sit in my prison cell, with a few hours of my last day in this world and I take the liberty to write these few lines to let you all know that I can meet it without fear....There is not one man in this country that has been brought up any better than me." After completing the letters, he composed a song and then lay down to sleep. At 1:00 a.m., he awoke and began singing and then went back to sleep until awoken by a jailer. Reverend Stevenson from the Presbyterian Church arrived early to sit with the doomed man. Together they prayed and sang up to the hour of his death. Clark had then eaten breakfast, showing what the *Chronicle* calls remarkable courage and indifference to his fate. Clark's execution would take place midmorning on January 1. At 11:10 a.m., Clark was taken from the cell, tightly bound, and led up the steps of the scaffold. It was said he posed himself as though for a photograph. The rope was put about his neck and the black hood adjusted but not pulled down before he spoke. His last words he spoke loud and clear:

> *Well, gentlemen, I suppose you all know what I am here for—at least you say that I am here for the murder of Thomas Rogers. Gentleman of Bozeman I stand here to-day, that I am an innocent man. I am innocent of the crime and I know nothing about it whatever. The man that testified against me has sworn falsely but I can meet my God an innocent man as far as this crime is concerned. My mother was brought up in good society. I was raised with a good pious mother and in one of the best families of the State where I came from, and now I will meet my God. Farewell to my Southern, sunny home, my loving mother and the one I love.*

Immediately following these last words, the black hood was pulled down by Sheriff Blakeley, and Jas. Ponsford, deputy sheriff, dropped the man to his death. He moved convulsively twice and then was motionless. Ten minutes later, the doctors felt no pulse, and Clark was taken to Undertaker Sennett for burial. According to the *Butte Miner*, his mother had been present, coming forward to kiss her son before the hood was placed; however, it seems this may have been an inaccuracy, for the *Bozeman Chronicle* never mentions her presence.[141]

The scaffold that ended Clark's life was originally constructed for Carl Adolphson, who had been convicted of murdering his partner, Andrew

Sheriff C.P. Blakley, 1883–85. *Gallatin Historical Society/Gallatin History Museum.*

Sioberg. According to one witness, Erick Peterson, the two business partners had been quarreling on the night of the murder about money matters. It seems Sioberg owed all the men at the cabin money. Charley Johnson, one of the men who stayed at the cabin that night, also quarreled with Sioberg, striking him three times with his hand during an argument. Adolphson had then thrown the man on the bed, saying he would "make his pain short before morning." Peterson had seen Sioberg get up about 2:30 a.m. to go outside; when he returned, he had asked Adolphson for more cover. That was when, Peterson testified, he saw Adolphson draw a knife across Sioberg's throat. He then testified that he heard the blood dripping but went back to sleep. The next morning, they had all gotten up to eat breakfast, following which Peterson discovered Sioberg was in a "dying condition." Peterson said Sioberg asked for coffee but did not drink any. However, according to Dr. Whitefoot, who examined Sioberg's body, the man's jugular and windpipe had both been severed, so it would have been impossible for him to have lived over thirty minutes. The coroner stated that Peterson testified at the coroner's inquest that Sioberg had committed suicide. Even at the trial, Peterson stated that Adolphson had said, "The scrub has lain there and cut himself" upon the discovery of Sioberg's condition.[142]

The *Independent Record*, which detailed the circumstances of the case, noted that while the evidence against Adolphson was damning, there was no doubt that Peterson had laid out contradictory statements. It was noted how strange it would have been for a man to see a murder committed and just go back to sleep. It was also noted that the night of Sioberg's death there had been no moon, according to the almanac, so there had been no way for Peterson to have seen a murder at all. In fact, the coroner noted a lamp had to be used during the daytime to see the corpse, as the cabin had only one tiny window. That paired with the fact that Sioberg could not have asked for coffee seemed to prove Peterson's testimony as false. The *Independent Record* stood firm with Adolphson, writing: "Should Adolphson be executed…there is little doubt that another crime will be added to the list in Montana."[143]

Adolphson was nevertheless convicted of the murder and sentenced to be hanged on August 24, 1883. Adolphson was in complete preparation to meet his death, keeping his Swedish Bible with him always; he was often visited by ministers and always swore his innocence. A respite was granted just a week prior to the execution date, and he was resentenced to February 7, 1884. The respite was granted due to an issue in hearing the appeal to the Supreme Court of Montana during that session. Soon a new trial was granted; however, it was widely believed that a conviction would be a near impossibility. The witnesses had all left town, possibly because one of them had been guilty of murder or at least perjury, and the Supreme Court did not believe the evidence at hand supported a guilty verdict. In any event, little was heard of the case again, and it seems Adolphson was at some point released as an innocent party. Thus, the gallows constructed for him lay in wait for John A. Clark.

On Wednesday, October 4, 1905, the *Great Falls Tribune* printed the headline "Chops Head of Sing Open: Brutal Murder of a Chinaman in Bozeman, Supposedly on Highbinder Orders." (A highbinder was an assassin, one who belonged to a Chinese American criminal organization.) According to the article, Tom Sing, proprietor of a laundry, was sitting at the butcher block of a restaurant eating his breakfast when Lu Sing came up behind him with a sharp hatchet and cut six gashes in Tom Sing's head. Lu Sing was immediately arrested for the crime and supposedly relieved and happy on the way to the jail when he was told Tom Sing was dead.[144]

The murder had occurred at ten o'clock in the morning on October 3. In one account, Lu Sing had first attempted his attack with a butcher knife but had been stopped by others in the kitchen, so he had resorted to the hatchet that he had found there. In a second account, he had hit Tom Sing three times with the hatchet, which had been in the room, and then grabbed the knife. When Tom Sing started to rise back up to his feet, Lu Sing hit him three more times with the hatchet instead. Reports stated the kitchen and adjoining premises were a mess. Tom Sing may have been moved to a more comfortable place where he died within ten minutes of receiving the blows. Many of the blows were said to have been fatal, one having penetrated the brain by a few inches.[145]

According to the paper, Tom Sing's wife, known as Na Lay (aka Anne Kum Chee), had been bought by Lu Sing in San Francisco as a young girl. She had been rescued and given an education by others, including Tom Sing, whom she had later married. Na Lay had been to San Francisco again but had recently returned to Bozeman, where she had been arrested due to

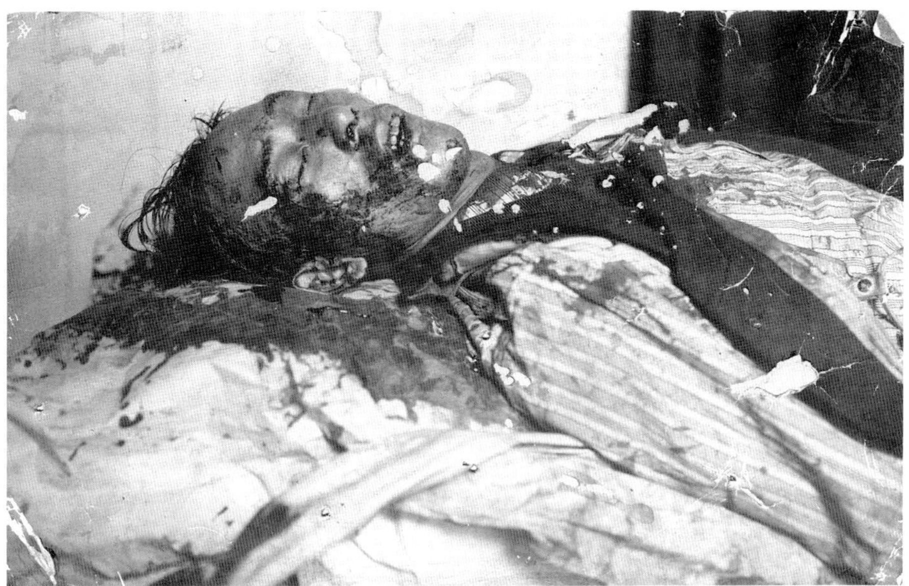

A dead man believed to be Tom Sing lying atop a blood-soaked bed. *Gallatin Historical Society/Gallatin History Museum.*

a lack of correct of paperwork to stay in the United States. It is unclear if her arrest had been prior to or following the death of her husband. It was possible Lu Sing had followed the couple to Montana, and it was muddy if he had been in the area for a year or simply a few months. The details were very blurry and would remain so for much of the case.[146]

A week later it was announced that Attorney J.L. Staats had been appointed to defend Lu Sing at his trial. That same paper gave details of a funeral that had been held for Tom Sing "with all the ceremonies of Chinese Freemasons." A short service had been first held at the Kay & Davis undertaking parlors, followed by a longer one in the street by Tom Sing's former laundry. There had been music and proceedings by a Chinese Freemason along with food that had been laid on a table at the foot of the casket. A similar ceremony was performed at the graveside as well. A band had accompanied the transfer from place to place, and those riding on the hearse scattered slips of paper that had been filled with holes "through which the devil is supposed to crawl before he can reach the deceased." Those not part of the Chinese community were in high attendance, watching the foreign ceremonies as though "witnessing a vaudeville show."[147]

Little would be mentioned about the case until November 10, 1905, when the results of the trial would be shared in the *Republican Courier*. The trial had not taken up a lot of time, just a few days had been concerned with questioning the witnesses and the decision of the jury. Yung Sing, proprietor of the restaurant where the murder had occurred, was the principal witness for the prosecution. According to Yung, he had been making pastry when he heard one of the blows from the hatchet. While he had not seen Lu Sing enact a blow, he had been first on the scene and had attempted to keep Lu from causing further damage to Tom by grabbing his hands, which had held a knife and a hatchet. Mar Quong had also been present at the scene and, like Yung, had only heard the blow and seen Lu with the knife and hatchet but had not seen an actual blow struck. Policeman Williams, first to arrest Lu Sing, testified to the latter having stated on the way to the city jail, "If me no kill him, me no good man; if Tom Sing dead, me die happy." The policeman had been called by Mrs. May Gilray, who had told him to "come quick or they will cut Tom Sing's head off."[148]

Chin Yuen testified through an interpreter that he and Lu Sing had been peeling potatoes that morning when he had left to build a fire to wash the dishes. He too heard the blows but did not see them, coming to help Yung hold Lu. He had taken the hatchet from him while the knife had fallen to the floor. According to the paper, his demonstration of the murder had made the jury extremely uncomfortable, as he had looked "very fierce and weird." According to Dr. Jump, out of the six gashes, three would have caused Tom to die. The jury and Lu Sing were taken to the kitchen during the trial to witness the scene of the crime.[149]

Lu Sing was put on the stand on his own behalf, stating that he remembered being in the restaurant but could not remember anything about the killing of Tom. According to the paper, "he clean forgot that part of it, but he did remember trying to take a cup of coffee to Tom Sing, when he saw him lying on the floor, but was prevented from doing this charitable act by Yung Sing and Chin Yeuen." Chin Yeuen was put back on the stand; he had not seen any cup of coffee in Lu Sing's hand. The *Republican Courier*'s position on the case was made very clear by the manner in which it reported Lu Sing's testimony about the coffee cup. It seems Lu Sing's fate was sealed, the jury bringing back a verdict of guilty of murder in the first degree.[150]

On Saturday, the day following the trial, Lu Sing was sentenced to death by Judge Stewart despite attempts to stall the sentencing by defense attorney Staats. Staats's objections were to the pronouncing of the sentence before the two-day-from-the-trial standard and that he believed the defendant to be insane. The objections were overruled, and a sentence proceeded as follows:

> *Lu Sing, you are about to be sentenced to death, and the awful situation in which you are at this time prompts the court to urge you to consider well the end of your life, which is rapidly approaching. I do not desire to comment upon your unhappy condition or the facts or circumstances which brought it about, further than to say that, in this case, the court believes that you have had a fair and impartial trial.…It is the judgement of the law and sentence of this court that you be remanded to the custody of the sheriff and be by him securely kept in close confinement until a certain day, hereafter to be designated, which day shall not be less than thirty days nor more than sixty days from this date, and that upon the said day the sheriff take you to some convenient place, as appointed and required by law, and there execute the sentence of this court, by causing you to be hanged by the neck until you are dead, dead, dead; and may God have mercy on your soul.*[151]

From the moment Lu Sing was returned to the jail to await his execution, a death watch was put in place, George Herndon during the day and Edward Scott during the night, to ensure Lu did not escape justice by his own hand. According to the paper, Lu made every effort to get out of the jail, trying to get past the guards when his food was brought to him. The realization of his fate had sunk in.[152]

The death warrant was received by Sheriff Ed Reynolds the following week, and Friday December 15 was set as the date. The hour would be chosen by the sheriff himself. Lu Sing was reported as being extremely nervous and jumpy. When having his photo taken, he told the sheriff that he was "going up through the sky" the next month. Lu was to wear American clothes until the date of his execution, when he would be dressed in Chinese attire. Later reports indicate he wore American clothes to the gallows instead.[153]

The motive for the brutal murder would remain a mystery. The only information available was a rumor that there had been a price put on Tom Sing's head in recent years. The rumor was close to the story of how Tom Sing had married his wife. From what officers could gather from the Chinese community, Tom Sing had "suited Mrs. Sing better than the other fellow and being in the land of the free and the brave, she married him." It was believed that those slighted in the dealings had put a sum of $600 on the head of Tom Sing shortly thereafter. If that was the case, the company who put up the sum never acknowledged Lu Sing's accomplishment. A different story was also circulated that Lu had eyes for Tom Sing's wife and thought removing Tom from the picture would do the trick. According to the *Republican Courier*, the Chinese community was confused why Lu Sing had not already been

Sheriff's Office,

Gallatin County, Montana

Bozeman, Mont,, April 7, 1906.

To Mr. Fred Lay

Bozeman Mont

You are hereby invited to attend the

Legal Execution of Lu Sing,

For the murder of Tom Sing on the

3rd day of October, 1905.

The execution will take place

in the jail yard in the City of Bozeman, Montana,

On Friday, the 20th day of April, 1906,

between the hours of 1 a. m. and 10 a. m.

E. M. Reynolds

Sheriff of Gallatin County.

An invitation to the execution of Lu Sing sent to local attorney Fred Lay by Sheriff E.M Reynolds. *Gallatin Historical Society/Gallatin History Museum.*

executed, many exclaiming, "If he lived in China he would have his head chopped off next day."[154]

According to an article published in the *Butte Daily Post* from April 1906, Na Lay had known that a price was on the head of any man she was found with. She had neglected to tell Tom of this situation but had told him to always eat his meals at home, thinking he might be attacked for the reward. When she arrived at his side following Lu Sing's attack, she had "stroked his cheeks and scolded him for not eating his breakfast at home."

The same paper also noted that prior to the murder, Lu Sing had asked Reverend M.L. Rickman for a letter to be addressed to San Francisco. When the reverend couldn't understand the name, he told Lu he should ask Tom Sing, to which Lu became agitated, stating that Tom was a bad man, before tearing up the letter. It was believed this letter may have been to those who had promoted the assassination.[155]

An appeal to the Supreme Court of Montana stalled the execution date just days before it was to occur. The *Republican Courier* again made its stance on the subject clear: "He may, of course, gain his freedom or a new trial, as technicalities often gain precedence over facts. No one doubts that Lu Sing was a cold-blooded murderer." It was said that over five thousand people had visited the jail to see the murderer.[156]

The appeal dragged on for some time, eventually coming back in the negative. On April 10, it was announced that Lu Sing was to be hanged on April 20, 1906. At the printing of the new execution date, it seems the motive of the killing now accepted as truth was that of an assassination. According to the *Republican Courier*, which seems to have received new information by this time, the assassin (Lu Sing) had been hired by a man who had owned Na Lay before Tom Sing had stolen her away in Astoria, Oregon. The hit was for a double assassination of both Tom Sing and his wife, but Lu Sing had been unable to get them together to accomplish the full deed.[157]

The gallows for the event were brought into the jail yard from Butte, the property of Silver Bow County. Invitations were mailed by Sheriff Reynolds to the jury members who had tried the case, local sheriffs in other counties, members of the press and a few citizens. The invitations were on mourning stationery with an image of Lu Sing in the corner. While the execution was to be private beyond the twelve needed for legal purposes as witnesses, the other invitations were at the discretion of the sheriff, and those invited in this case were quite the customary group.[158]

Days later, it was noted that Lu Sing had gone on a food strike. He had stopped voluntarily eating and drinking, but that had not stopped the department from keeping his strength up. It was noted that once a day the deputies and those on death watch "place Lu Sing on the floor, pry open and pour soup into his mouth, then hold his nose tight until the dose is swallowed." While he fought "like a bulldog," it seems he was no match for those in the department. It was noted on occasion this was done twice a day when they had the time, but that it was "pretty hard work to tackle."[159]

The next report of Lu Sing was following his execution. Shortly after one o'clock in the morning on April 20, Lu Sing paid for his crime. The newspaper reported that the "decently conducted" execution had been witnessed by 150 people, all men except for two women who were young local waitresses. However, details of the execution show it was anything but decent. At one o'clock, Sheriff Reynolds, Undersheriff Sales and several deputies went to the cell of Lu Sing to read him the death warrant, which was then repeated by an interpreter to the condemned man. While Lu was said to have been trembling, he gave no trouble when those present adjusted straps that were to hold his arms and legs close to his body. While going up the stairs into the jail yard Lu became faint and had to be held up for a bit. It was said that he hadn't really realized what was to happen that day. When officers came for him, it was said that he told them about someone coming to help him. It seems he had not truly understood that his hour had come; the case was finished.[160]

Five minutes later, the group was standing underneath the gallows, illuminated by an electric light, with a noose adjusted around Lu Sing's neck. The interpreter asked if Lu had anything he wished to say, to which Lu responded and the interpreter shared with the crowd: "I wanted to give Tom Sing cup of coffee. I saw Tom Sing and the cleaver, then cloud went over my eyes. Then Tom Sing was lying by meat block. I want to notify my cousin in Butte. I want to notify you people that I never killed anyone." The black cap was drawn over his head, and on the sheriff's cue, an unknown man beneath a blanket shielding him from sight released a 320-pound weight that jerked Lu Sing up off the ground by his neck. For the next fifteen minutes, his body continued to tremble; at ten minutes, the body began to squirm, his pulse growing stronger for a bit before slowing until he was finally pronounced dead. This seems to have been anything but "decent." Three minutes after being pronounced dead, Lu Sing was cut down and placed in a coffin that was buried in the local cemetery just before daylight.[161]

Reports at the time do not really show the emotional state of the community during this time. Seventeen years later, in 1924, in the appeal process of Seth Danner, condemned to die for first-degree murder, local

Mignor Quaw Lott touched on the subject, stating, "I know what a fearful effect it [execution] has upon a community. At that time, the gentlest people were temporarily transformed into bloodthirsty animals."[162] The *Butte Daily Post* reported the execution as a "grewsome scene," stating that Lu died from fifteen minutes of strangulation, not a broken neck. It was noted that those witnessing stormed the gallows after, cutting pieces of the rope as a souvenir. The crowd had been broken up by officers when then it had started to break pieces off the gallows.[163]

The tragedy did not end there. Na Lay, Tom Sing's wife, was in danger of being deported due to a lack of paperwork permitting her to live and work in the United States. On March 15, 1906, it was reported in the *Anaconda Standard* that a federal court had made the decision that she had to be sent back to China. According to reports, she was in a "dangerous and peculiar position." Tom Sing had left debts unpaid and no will. Na Lay had gone to work at his laundry right away, attempting to pay the debts, but as a noncitizen, she was in a precarious situation. To compound the issue, she was frightened to go back to China, as she believed those who had caused her husband's death would come after her there. It was believed she had been placed in the jail so as not to harm herself due to this fear. Unfortunately, she was confined just thirty feet from her husband's killer, Lu Sing. At one point, Deputy Sheriff Bull found her crying at the jail, and when asked what the matter was, she said that the world was so big and she was a little girl.[164]

It was during this time that a law called the Chinese Exclusion Act passed that unfairly targeted those of Asian background who wished to enter the United States. According to the *Republican Courier*, there had been 165,540 alien arrivals in New York, a good percentage of them having come from Italy. It was noted that one-quarter of this grouping could not read or write. While all these people were allowed to come to America, those of Asian descent were meticulously tracked down and sent back. The paper was angry that so many criminals were set free into our land but that Na Lay, who was educated and an industrious member of this community, was to be sent back at government expense and with heartache. As the paper noted, "she was found guilty of having been brought to this country during her minority, without her connivance or consent, and that through no fault of her own, she happened to be minus the necessary documents showing that she was rightfully entitled to residence here." While the writer did not think the law unjust, the way in which peculiar circumstances were not considered was.[165]

On March 25, it was announced that there had been a meeting of prominent citizens and businessmen in Bozeman to consider the deportation of Na Lay. It was decided that a stay of deportation be asked for in Helena to grant them twenty days for Reverend R.M. Donaldson to go to Washington and President Roosevelt on her behalf. It was noted that she had come to this country as a small child and to send her back would be to send her to "a foreign country, where she would be friendless and penniless."[166] Days later it was printed that she had been released from the jail under bond and on appeal. Her intention was to find work as a domestic with a family in Bozeman as she feared going back to work at the laundry because she believed a man belonging to the same company as Lu Sing was in the city. According to the *Anaconda Standard*, it had been reported that she had offered $1,000 to any American that would marry her, but this proved to be a false report after she received and refused three proposals; however, it was noted that she had "many callers in the jail."[167] It is unknown what became of Na Lay following this tragedy in her life, but one hopes she found peace and quiet working in a Bozeman home.

Mrs. Tom Sing, Who Was Ordered Deported to China.

Mrs. Tom Sing (Na Lay). *From the* Butte Miner, *March 28, 1906, Newspapers.com.*

Seventeen years later, local citizens would again experience a shocking murder and the aftermath of conviction. On June 9, 1923, those living in the Gallatin Valley woke up to a shocking headline: "Conscience-Stricken Wife Tells of Husband's Brutal Murders." Almost instantly, a relatively unknown family became the news of the year. Mrs. Iva Danner had confessed that her husband had murdered two people in the fall of 1920. Her accusation had been given weight when two bodies were found buried in a shallow grave in Central Park. Her husband, Seth Danner, was brought into custody, and the saga of his life began to come to light. The dramatized storytelling of the newspapers would condemn him for the crimes far before the jury, but this would be just the tip of the iceberg. Along with racial profiling (due to his supposed Cherokee blood), Seth was accused of robbing Iva's innocence and committing incest and had his head examined in a phrenology test that determined his mental capacity was that of an underdeveloped prehistoric man. He would even be suspected of murders that occurred long before he was in the area. Despite all this prying and speculation, little was known about the real man.

Seth was born in Kansas on May 15, 1882. It seems he spent time with his uncle Bert, enough that when Bert suddenly died in an accident, Seth soon after married his dead uncle's wife, Nancy. They were only a few years apart in age. With this marriage, Seth became stepfather to his niece, Iva Danner. He had three children with Nancy, one named Florence, before Nancy's death in 1915. Iva possibly went to live with an uncle at this point but not for long. In December 1916, Seth and Iva were married in Dillon, Montana; Iva's first child was born the next day. One story claims that Iva had Seth come get her because she was "in a bad way" and that the child was not his. In Dillon, however, he was forced to marry her by the town or be locked up in jail.

Times were hard, but Seth usually found work as a mechanic in between the threshing seasons. As a result, the family led a nomadic life, moving with the harvest from South Dakota to Montana and back again. In the fall of 1920, the Danners left Mobridge, South Dakota, planning to settle back in Montana for a spell. They made the trip with Seth's daughter Florence; their two young children, Della and Marvin; and a married couple, John and Florence Sprouse. The Sprouses had no children and were slightly older than the Danners. Together they camped at Central Park, Montana, in tents, living off the land and hunting and trapping in the marshes around the area. Locals knew of the tent camp, but neither couple socialized much with anyone. Very few had spoken to them. In November 1920, the Danners moved to Three Forks, and the Sprouses disappeared.

Three years later, in April 1923, Seth Danner and a man named Seagraves were picked up on a moonshine charge. While inspecting his living quarters, the police found an engine that matched one stolen elsewhere, and Seth was booked on a grand larceny charge as well. He was sentenced to ten years at the state prison in Deer Lodge but was paroled to provide for his family. He was forced to get a job in Bozeman as a mechanic. He would visit Iva and the children occasionally on his motorcycle but mostly wrote letters to his wife.

It was during this time of physical separation that Iva reportedly felt safe to come forward with her story of the 1920 murders. She first contacted the Three Forks police. They were unable to locate anything, but her persistence brought in Bozeman sheriff Jim Smith. Together, the Three Forks police, Sheriff Smith and Iva uncovered the bodies. However, the Sheriff's Department must have found Iva's story credible even without the evidence

Florence Sprouse and John Sprouse, as published in the *Bozeman Courier*, October 31, 1923. *Gallatin Historical Society/Gallatin History Museum.*

of the crime, as Seth was taken into custody the night before the bodies were found, on the evening of June 7. Seth happened to be in Three Forks when he was picked up, not knowing the charge. Interestingly, Seth drove his own motorcycle, and the deputy rode in the sidecar. They arrived at the jail about midnight. In his first comments, he stated he had not seen the Sprouses since South Dakota. This would prove to be detrimental to his case.

Before Iva could be a witness in a murder trial, she had to get a divorce from Seth. At first, the case looked good for Seth, but it quickly deteriorated as members of the community stepped forward to tell how they had provided the Danner children with food, clothes, shoes and shelter. Iva's stories of Seth's brutality brought the case to a close in August, and Iva was granted a divorce. The children, now totaling four including Florence, were shuffled about some, but ultimately ended up at the Twin Bridges orphanage, as Seth could not receive custody and Iva did not want them.

The murder trial was held from October 22 to 26. Young Florence Danner would be brought back as a key witness during the trial but was unable to say anything on the stand. She had been told to stay quiet by one of the parents; it will never be known which. Two stories came out as to what happened. Iva gave hers on the stand, while Seth's was an affidavit that was read in full. Seth did not take the stand.

According to Iva's story, John and Seth had been out trapping one day when Seth came back alone. As night fell, Florence Sprouse grew anxious, but Seth told her he had left John in the afternoon and had no idea where he'd gone. As Florence's anxiety grew, Iva claims that Seth hit her in the head with an axe, saying, "I reckon she'll know where Jack is now."[168] He then tied a string around her neck to make her suffocate to death. That night, he went and got John and placed him in the tent next to Florence. According to Iva, Seth had killed John earlier with a shotgun blast to the head. He showed the bodies to Iva, warning her never to tell, and then buried them the next night. The motive, according to Iva, was robbery.

Seth's story conversely stated that Florence and John had been out checking traps, as there had been a row between the women and it was determined they were not to be left alone together. Seth had been away from camp but in a different direction. He came back to camp in time to see Florence Sprouse pointing a gun at Iva. There was a struggle, which Seth became a part of, and before he could stop her, Iva hit Florence in the head with a hatchet. Death was not instantaneous, but Florence never regained consciousness. The next day, Seth went out and found John, who had been killed with a shotgun blast to the head. Tracks had been easy to follow in a skiff of snow. According to Seth, Florence had seen Iva and John in the brush together and, in her rage, took John out and killed him and then came back for Iva. Seth told Iva she should confess to self-defense, but she refused. So he buried the two bodies. Part of his story included a mention of the gun catching on Florence's finger in the struggle, pulling back a large piece of her skin. Much of his story included details, while Iva's story very rarely deterred from simple facts. Either Seth was a great storyteller, or the details were real.

The jury was out for seven hours, and four votes were taken. Never once was there a doubt in the jurors' mind as to his guilt. The multiple votes were in deciding his fate. Seth was found guilty and sentenced to execution by hanging.

The execution was to occur on January 11, 1924. Following the trial, there were multiple articles written that discussed the bias of the jury. No one could deny that every member of the jury had known something about the case prior to the trial. One juryman, William Heaston, in particular was scrutinized as having stated multiple times that he would hang Danner no matter what because it would be "getting rid of rubbish."[169] Interestingly, this same man would be sent to Deer Lodge prison as a seventy-nine-year-old convicted of murder. (He was paroled a year later due to his age.) Since the Danners and Sprouses were transient folks, it seems that it was the opinion of many that no good could come of them and that Seth was no doubt guilty.

In November 1923, Iva married Jim Troglia, a local baker who had helped her and the family during their time in the area. Seth was reportedly delighted; he thought her dismissal of the children and quick marriage was evidence of her guilt.

On January 10, 1924, the 110,000-word transcript of the trial was submitted to the Supreme Court of Montana for an appeal, immediately granting Seth a stay of execution. In the meantime, a new ring had been installed in the 1911 execution mechanism, probably because Seth was a large man. The gallows at the Gallatin County jail were part of local architect Fred Willson's design for the building and were manufactured by the Diebold Safe Company.

Throughout Seth's time in the jail, much was written about his eating habits and his spirits. It was noted that Seth was excited to have Jim Smith's wife back from vacation, as the meals would be proper again. During the trial, Iva had lived in the women's cells; she could come and go as she pleased but spent nights there, held as a witness. She could hear Seth playing his banjo down below in his cell and seemed anxious to be near him. Seth spent his birthday in the jail, and a party was thrown, complete with a cake made by local ladies. He spent most of his time, especially while on "death watch" talking to the guards about philosophy and religion. It seems he was not the uneducated man people had made him out to be.

Before and after the stay of execution, letters were written to the governor in behalf of Seth Danner asking for life imprisonment instead. Many were from religious groups and local women. A few letters were from his two sisters. One, a Mrs. Mabel Moody of Oregon, visited Seth in the spring of 1924, having not seen him since they were children. She wrote to the governor: "When I was in Bozeman, when I went to the jail to see my bro, I had to walk under that gallows, in my mind I can see him day or night hanging at the end of that rope. Gladly I would take his place if I could."[170] In the end, the Montana Supreme Court found there was no mistrial, and a new execution date was set of July 18, 1924.

Seth Orrin Danner. *Gallatin Historical Society/Gallatin History Museum.*

Shortly after midnight on July 18, Seth was baptized by two Catholic priests, one from Bozeman and the other from Livingston. At 2:08 a.m., the "death march" started from the isolation cells. At the gallows, Sheriff Smith saw to the adjusting of the arm and leg straps before asking: "Dan, have you got anything to say?" Seth stated: "I want to tell you people that I hold no malice against any man. I have made peace with my God, and will go to him knowing that I am fully prepared; and I would like to see each and every one of you people to follow my example. I have nothing more to say. Good bye, one and all."[171]

The hood was placed, the trap sprung and his death was instantaneous at 2:19 a.m. The body was taken down after fifteen minutes and laid in a coffin that was immediately taken to the Catholic cemetery for a flashlight burial. The last execution in Gallatin County.

When one relates one case to another, one can't help but wonder why some men paid the ultimate price, while others were allowed to live, sometimes even to regain their freedom. Was it due to the caliber of the defense or prosecution? Or the bias of the jury, or the prominence of the person accused? When one looks at each case, one must think, were they guilty? Sometimes the answer is yes. But if it's not, are there more unsolved crimes among us, more ghosts of the wrongly accused?

NOTES

Chapter 1

1. "Enraged Workman Is Jess Crago's Slayer," *Weekly Courier* (Bozeman, MT), August 20, 1913.
2. "Murder in the First Degree for Domenico Romeo," *Weekly Courier* (Bozeman, MT), August 27, 1913.
3. "Self-Defense Is Plea on Behalf D. Romeo," *Weekly Courier* (Bozeman, MT), October 8, 1913.
4. "Romeo Case Is Postponed," *Weekly Courier* (Bozeman, MT), November 19, 1913.
5. "Italian Is Guilty of Second Degree Murder," *Weekly Courier* (Bozeman, MT), December 16, 1913.
6. "Italian Given 40 Year Term," *Weekly Courier* (Bozeman, MT), December 17, 1913.
7. "Little Progress Toward Clearing the Mystery," *Butte Miner* (Butte, MT), December 28, 1915.
8. "Joe Reiser, Fugitive Partner of Slain Salesville Man, Captured," *Butte Miner* (Butte, MT), January 1, 1916.
9. "Reiser Confesses His Pal's Murder," *Great Falls Tribune* (Great Falls, MT), January 4, 1916.
10. Ibid.
11. "Reiser Tells Bloody Story," *Great Falls Tribune* (Great Falls, MT), February 25, 1916.

12. "Murderer Sentenced," *Great Falls Tribune* (Great Falls, MT), February 29, 1916.
13. "Two Found Dead in Gallatin Canyon," *Butte Miner* (Butte, MT), February 1, 1917.
14. "Andrew Levinski Surrenders to Officer," *Butte Miner* (Butte, MT), February 2, 1917.
15. "Bozeman News," *Anaconda Standard* (Anaconda, MT), February 12, 1917.
16. "For Killing Two Men Levenski Is Facing His Jury," *Weekly Courier* (Bozeman, MT), June 13, 1917.
17. Ibid.
18. "For Dual Killing Andrew Levenski Excused by Jury," *Weekly Courier* (Bozeman MT), June 20, 1917.
19. "France Huffine Wounded in Quarrel with a Ranch Hand," *Bozeman Courier* (Bozeman, MT), January 21, 1920.
20. Ibid.
21. "Nunnelly Out on Large Bond," *Bozeman Courier* (Bozeman, MT), February 11, 1920.
22. "Nunnelly Freed by Jury Verdict," *Bozeman Courier* (Bozeman, MT), March 10, 1920.
23. Ibid.
24. "Slining, Shipman Go on Trial for Murder in First Degree," *Bozeman Courier* (Bozeman, MT), June 5, 1931.
25. "Slining and Shipman to Be Tried on Charge of First Degree Murder," *Bozeman Courier* (Bozeman, MT), June 1931.
26. "Slining, Shipman Go on Trial for Murder in First Degree."
27. "Clostad Slayers Will Serve Long Term in the Pen," *Bozeman Courier* (Bozeman, MT), June 12, 1931.
28. "Shot in Head on Ranch Near Gallatin Gateway on Sunday," *Bozeman Courier* (Bozeman, MT), September 7, 1934.
29. Ibid.
30. "Holland Case Will Go to Jury Shortly," *Daily Inter Lake* (Kalispel, MT), November 17, 1934.
31. "Aged Slayer Is Given Life at Bozeman," *Great Falls Tribune* (Great Falls, MT), November 24, 1934.

Chapter 2

32. "A Fatal Gun Play," *Bozeman Courier* (Bozeman, MT), July 23, 1898.
33. Ibid.
34. Ibid.
35. "Gets Fifteen Years," *Anaconda Standard* (Anaconda, MT), December 9, 1898,
36. "Double Tragedy at Belgrade," *Avant Courier* (Bozeman, MT), January 20, 1900.
37. Ibid.
38. "Rogers' Love Was Blind," *Anaconda Standard* (Anaconda, MT), January 16, 1900.
39. Ibid.
40. Ibid.
41. Ibid.
42. Ibid.
43. "Triple Tragedy," *Avant Courier* (Bozeman, MT), September 15, 1900.
44. "Terrible Tragedy," *Butte Miner* (Butte, MT), September 11, 1900.
45. "Last Week's Triple Tragedy in Peaceful Park County," *Anaconda Standard* (Anaconda, MT), September 16, 1900.
46. Ibid.
47. Ibid.
48. Ibid.
49. "Husband Shoots Twice and Wife Was the Victim," *Weekly Courier* (Bozeman, MT), December 8, 1915.
50. "Saw Accused Shoot Woman," *Great Falls Tribune* (Great Falls, MT), February 16, 1916.
51. "Anderson Relates Story of Shooting," *Anaconda Standard* (Anaconda, MT), February 18, 1916.
52. Ibid.
53. "Anderson Found Guilty; 10 Years," *Great Falls Tribune* (Great Falls, MT), February 20, 1916.

Chapter 3

54. "Body Found in Madison Above Three Forks Thought That of Harry Walker," *Bozeman Courier* (Bozeman, MT), July 7, 1920.

55. "Murder of Harry Walker Charged to Act of Laura Adams of Three Forks," *Bozeman Courier* (Bozeman, MT), January 4, 1922.
56. "Mystery Grows Deeper as New Facts Develop," *Anaconda Standard* (Anaconda, MT), January 4, 1922.
57. "Gallatin Woman Held for Murder," *Augusta News* (Augusta, MT), January 12, 1922.
58. Ibid.
59. "Three Forks Woman Freed of All Charges in Connection with Death of Harry Walker," *Butte Miner* (Butte, MT), March 12, 1922.

Chapter 4

60. "Death by Poison," *Avant Courier* (Bozeman, MT), October 12, 1901.
61. Ibid.
62. Ibid.
63. "Poisoned to Death!," *Avant Courier* (Bozeman, MT), October 19, 1901.
64. Ibid.
65. "The Poisoning Case," *Avant Courier* (Bozeman, MT), October 26, 1901.
66. "The Mrs. John Black Murder Case," *Avant Courier* (Bozeman, MT), November 30, 1901.
67. "Black Murder Case," *Avant Courier* (Bozeman, MT), February 7, 1901.
68. Ibid.
69. Ibid.
70. Ibid.
71. Ibid.
72. Ibid.
73. "Mrs. Lucy Black Sentenced," *Avant Courier* (Bozeman, MT), February 21, 1902.
74. "More Evidences of the Poisoning," *Anaconda Standard* (Anaconda, MT), February 7, 1902.
75. "An Illogical Verdict," *Anaconda Standard* (Anaconda, MT), February 14, 1902.
76. "Another Murder," *Republican-Courier* (Bozeman, MT), September 15, 1905.
77. Ibid.
78. "Witness in Murder Case Taken to Warm Springs," *Butte Miner* (Butte, MT), October 3, 1905.
79. "Purcell Found Guilty," *Republican-Courier* (Bozeman, MT), October 27, 1905.

80. "James Deskin Held in Jail Charged with Kelly Murder," *Bozeman Courier* (Bozeman, MT), September 28, 1934.
81. "Deskin on Trial on Shooting and Death Wm. Kelly," *Bozeman Courier* (Bozeman, MT), November 23, 1934.
82. Ibid.
83. "Deskin Gets Life Sentence for Shooting Wm. Kelly," *Bozeman Courier* (Bozeman, MT), November 30, 1934.
84. Ibid.
85. "Officers Search for Woman Who Vanished," *Independent Record* (Helena, MT), August 18, 1941.
86. "Body Found May Be That of Missing Three Forks Woman," *Daily Inter Lake* (Kalispel, MT), August 19, 1941.
87. "Slayer Hunt Is Continued," *Billings Gazette* (Billings, MT), August 22, 1941.
88. "Farm Worker Nabbed; Admits Slaying Three Forks Woman," *Havre Daily News* (Havre, MT), August 23, 1941.
89. "Three Forks Slaying Confessed," *Independent Record* (Helena, MT), August 23, 1941.
90. "Stallings Denies Connection with Murder at Salt Lake City," *Independent Record* (Helena, MT), August 30, 1941.
91. "Oral Confession Read to Jury," *Montana Standard* (Butte, MT), October 17, 1941.
92. Trial brief, *State of Montana v. Calvert Stallings*, Gallatin History Museum Archives.
93. "District Court Jury Convicts Eddie Stallings," *Missoulian* (Missoula, MT), October 20, 1941.
94. "Stallings, Calvert #13268," descriptive list of prisoner, Montana Memory Project, accessed April 30, 2021, mtmemory.org/digital/collection/p103401coll11/id/35067.

Chapter 5

95. "Fred Rogers Killed Without Warning by Richard Ward," *Bozeman Courier* (Bozeman, MT), November 12, 1919.
96. Ibid.
97. Ibid.
98. Ibid.
99. "Insanity Is Plea at the Ward Trial," *Bozeman Courier* (Bozeman, MT), January 21, 1920.

100. "One Man on Jury Saves Murderer," *Billings Gazette* (Billings, MT), January 24, 1920.
101. "Richard Ward Given Long Sentence Guilty of Murder of Fred Rogers," *Bozeman Courier* (Bozeman, MT), January 28, 1920.
102. "$3.40 Murderer Gets Long Term," *Billings Weekly Gazette* (Billings, MT), January 29, 1920.
103. Richard Ward and Willie Ward, Ancestry.com, accessed April 30, 2021, https://www.ancestry.com/search/?name=Richard_Ward&event=1920_bozeman-gallatin-montana-usa_56514&count=50&location=2&priority=usa.
104. "Fred Dambres Kills His Own Son in Insane Shooting Affray Monday," *Bozeman Courier* (Bozeman, MT), November 26, 1919.
105. Ibid.
106. Ibid.
107. "Dambres Will Be Tried on Sanity Before Facing Charge of Murder," *Bozeman Courier* (Bozeman, MT), January 28, 1920.
108. "Jury Charges Kunze Killed Mayor, Wife," *Great Falls Tribune* (Great Falls, MT), June 3, 1938.
109. "Sheriff Says Half Brother Killed Couple," *Billings Gazette* (Billings, MT), June 2, 1938.
110. Ibid.
111. "Kunze Is Now on Trial for Murder of Half Brother," *Independent-Record* (Helena, MT), October 11, 1938.
112. "Kunze Insane, Says Murder Trial Witness," *Great Falls Tribune* (Great Falls, MT), October 12, 1938.
113. "John Kunze Given a Life Sentence," *Daily Inter Lake* (Kalispell, MT), October 24, 1938.

Chapter 6

114. "Two Desperate Men," *Anaconda Standard* (Anaconda, MT), January 18, 1897.
115. Ibid.
116. "With Poor Success," *Anaconda Standard* (Anaconda, MT), January 21, 1897.
117. "Outlaws at Large," *Anaconda Standard* (Anaconda, MT), January 28, 1897.
118. Ibid.

119. "Funeral of Deputy Allen," *Anaconda Standard* (Anaconda, MT), February 8, 1897.
120. "He Got 80 Years," *Butte Daily Post* (Butte, MT), March 29, 1898.
121. "How the Girl Won Parole," *Butte Daily Post* (Butte, MT), January 29, 1910.
122. "Marshal Is Slain," *Missoulian* (Missoula, MT), January 28, 1915.
123. "Frank Durham Out on $35,000 Bail," *Butte Miner* (Butte, MT), February 13, 1915.
124. "Frank Durham Tried for Dolan Murder," *Anaconda Standard* (Anaconda, MT), April 1, 1915.
125. Ibid.
126. "Dolan's Reputation Good Say Some, Bad Say Others," *Anaconda Standard* (Anaconda, MT), April 3, 1915.
127. "Bozeman News," *Butte Miner* (Butte, MT), April 16, 1915.
128. "Bad Man Kills Two Deputies; Himself Slain," *Anaconda Standard* (Anaconda, MT), October 11, 1919.
129. Ibid.
130. Ibid.
131. "Triple Tragedy at Manhattan," *Bozeman Courier* (Bozeman, MT), October 15, 1919.
132. "New Lights on Murder Story," *Bozeman Courier* (Bozeman, MT), October 22, 1919.
133. Ibid.
134. "Triple Tragedy at Manhattan," *Bozeman Courier* (Bozeman, MT), October 15, 1919.
135. Ibid.
136. Francis L. Niven, "The Gallatin Valley's Most Gruesome Murders," Gallatin History Museum Archives.

Chapter 7

137. "Clark Hanged," *Bozeman Weekly Chronicle* (Bozeman, MT), January 1, 1884.
138. Ibid.
139. Ibid.
140. Ibid.
141. Ibid.
142. "Montana Justice," *Independent Record* (Helena, MT), January 27, 1884.
143. Ibid.

144. "Chops Head of Sing Open," *Great Falls Tribune* (Great Falls, MT), October 4, 1905.
145. "Cold Blooded Murder," *Republican-Courier* (Bozeman, MT), October 3, 1905.
146. Ibid.
147. "A Chinese Funeral," *Republican-Courier* (Bozeman, MT), October 10, 1905.
148. "Murder in First Degree," *Republican-Courier* (Bozeman, MT), November 10, 1905.
149. Ibid.
150. Ibid.
151. "His Time Is Short," *Republican-Courier* (Bozeman, MT), November 14, 1905.
152. Ibid.
153. "Death Warrant," *Republican-Courier* (Bozeman, MT), November 17, 1905.
154. Ibid.
155. "Lu Sing Swings to His Death," *Butte Daily Post* (Butte, MT), April 20, 1906.
156. "Has Appealed," *Republican-Courier* (Bozeman, MT), December 12, 1905.
157. "Lu Sing to Hang," *Republican-Courier* (Bozeman, MT), April 10, 1906.
158. Ibid.
159. *Republican-Courier* (Bozeman, MT), April 13, 1906.
160. "Lu Sing Is Dead," *Republican-Courier* (Bozeman, MT), April 20, 1906.
161. Ibid.
162. Mignor Quaw Lott to Governor Dixon, July 10, 1924, Montana Governor's Papers, MC35, Box 255, Folder 15, Montana Historical Society.
163. "Lu Sing Swings to His Death," *Butte Daily Post* (Butte, MT), April 20, 1906.
164. "Bad Dope for Mrs. Sing," *Anaconda Standard* (Anaconda, MT), March 15, 1906.
165. "Unjust Immigration Laws," *Republican-Courier* (Bozeman, MT), April 6, 1906.
166. "Will Appeal to President," *Anaconda Standard* (Anaconda, MT), March 26, 1906.
167. "Mrs. Tom Sing Is Made Happy," *Anaconda Standard* (Anaconda, MT), March 28, 1906.

168. "Mrs. Danner Holds Up Under Grueling Cross-Examination," *Bozeman Courier* (Bozeman, MT), October 24, 1923.
169. "Jurors Swear Danner Given Unbiased Trial," local paper (title unknown) (Bozeman, MT), 1923.
170. Mabel Moody to Governor Dixon, January 2, 1924, Montana Governor's Papers, MC35, Box 255, Folder 15, Montana Historical Society.
171. "Hangman's Noose Claims Danner for Murder of Mrs. John Sprouse," *Bozeman Courier* (Bozeman, MT), July 23, 1923.

INDEX

P

R

S

T

V

W

Drew Carter, photographer.

ABOUT THE AUTHOR

Kelly Hartman was raised in Silver Gate, Montana, attending kindergarten through eighth grade at the one-room schoolhouse in Cooke City. She received her associate of arts degree in art at Northwest Community College in Powell, Wyoming, and her bachelor of fine arts degree in painting from Western Oregon University in Monmouth, Oregon. She started her museum career as the director of the Cooke City, Montana Museum during its opening year. In 2016, she began work as the curator of the Gallatin History Museum in Bozeman, Montana. The museum is housed in the old county jail, where many of the prisoners in *Murder & Mayhem in Gallatin County, Montana* did time. Her books include *A Brief History of Cooke City* (2019), *Murder Along the Yellowstone Trail: The Execution of Seth Danner* (2020) and *Wicked Bozeman* (2021).

Visit us at
www.historypress.com